# GLORY DAYS

# MIDLAND ::RED:: D

Mike Greenwood

IAN ALLAN Publishing

*Front cover:*
No 3704 (NHA 704), a 1950 BMMO S10 with Metro-Cammell bodywork, passes Stoughton Church on a sunny spring morning in May 1966. Surprisingly it had just received a complete repaint even though other members of the class were being withdrawn. No 3704 was to last just another seven months in service
*Chris Aston*

*Back cover:*
Amongst the last service buses delivered to Midland Red was Leyland National 2 No 813 (BVP 813V). Photographed        e 1981, it is l        n Shrewsh        carryin        Analy          ure 'Ho               dentity.
*Mc*

*        uge:*
    .IA 223 was a 1938 Brush-bodied SOS FEDD. Seen in Burton-on-Trent bus station, one wonders whether the Old Judge Tea had any impact on the Uttoxeter car murder verdict!
*Peter Yeomans*

# Contents

First published 1998

ISBN 0 7110 2589 4

© Ian Allan Publishing Ltd 1998

Published by Ian Allan Publishing
an imprint of Ian Allan Publishing Ltd, Terminal House, Station Approach, Shepperton  Surrey TW17 8AS.
P  nted by  Ian Allan Printing Ltd at its works at Riverdene Business Park,
        ersham, Surrey KT12 4RG

# Introduction

To many, the Midland Red bus company had no peers. Not only did it become the largest bus company outside the metropolis, but its policy of building its own vehicles in volume remains unique and perhaps it is this that sets it aside from the other large bus operators. When one further considers the achievements the company made in vehicle development, often way ahead of its commercial competitors, the story is even more remarkable. Although Midland Red was massive in size, it still seemed capable of relating to all, and over time was held in true affection by many people: its own staff, the travelling public and enthusiasts alike. Indeed, the strap line 'The friendly Midland Red' was used for many years on all manner of publicity with good reason. However, one also has to acknowledge that during its long 77-year history many days were far from glorious!

This album is offered as a tribute and celebration of the entire Midland Red fleet and to the photographers who recorded the comings and goings over the years. The summary fleet list shows the rich variety of machinery that plied the company's routes. My gratitude goes to Paul Gray and John Seale of the Birmingham and Midland Motor Omnibus Trust (BaMMOT), who did much sterling work in researching the history of the company and identifying the early fleet, for allowing me to republish their findings. Peter Jacques of the Kithead Trust also responded promptly to my request for statistical data which follows the fleet summary and which also makes for interesting reading.

The first decision that had to be made when formulating the book was the period of coverage. The publishers took the easier decision that they wanted the book to start at the formation of the Midland Red Company, in 1904, but I had a number of choices of when to end the story! It could have been 1970 when the last BMMO-built vehicle entered service, 1973 when a substantial part of the company passed into the ownership of the West Midlands Passenger Transport Executive, or even 1974 when the last of the infamous 'HA' registration letters were used, but I quickly decided to choose 5 September 1981 when the Midland Red Omnibus Company ceased operation and was split into five separate units.

I have endeavoured to use, as much as possible, previously unpublished photographs and the selection of shots to represent well over 6,000 vehicles has resulted in much soul-searching in trying to get the balance right! My criterion, wherever possible, was to aim for the highest quality photography. If this also resulted in a rare vehicle being illustrated, so much the better. It perhaps comes as no surprise that the prewar fleet is covered only by black and white photographs whilst the postwar fleet is represented in glorious colour. The author is always keen to hear, via the publishers, of anyone who has previously unseen Midland Red material in colour or black and white, especially pre-1960s. Fortunately two of the country's most highly regarded bus photographers — Geoff Atkins and Tom Moore — included Midland Red amongst their favourite fleets and kindly allowed me access to their extensive collections. Add to these two gentlemen the well-known names of Malcolm Keeley and Geoff Lumb, plus the quality work of a number of new names, the opportunity afforded by Mike Jordan to search through the BaMMOT Midland Red photographic archive and the permission given to publish material recently made available by the Omnibus Society, and the result is a real treasury of images.

One of the delights of collecting photographs is the discovery of vintage material, and indeed one or two photographs used have only recently surfaced some 60 or 70 years after being taken! I hope the reader gains as much pleasure with the finished product as I have had in making the final selection.

Whilst compiling this book it is perhaps rather appropriate that 1998 marks the 75th anniversary of the first BMMO-built vehicle. Those of you who hanker after the good old days of Midland Red are strongly recommended to visit the Birmingham & Midland Museum of Transport situated at Wythall, on the outskirts of south Birmingham, which has become the spiritual home of preserved Midland Red vehicles. The Aston Manor Road Transport Museum in Birmingham also has a fine collection of former Midland Red vehicles and if you are fortunate to pick the right occasion you might be able to travel between the two sites by a preserved Midland Red bus!

*Mike*
Sheffield, March 1998

◀◀ An intriguing photograph of (OE 6170), a 1920 Tilling-Stevens TS3, believed to be taken at the Birmingham Railway Carriage & Wagon bodyshops. The Tilling-Stevens chassis was very popular with Midland Red in the early years with the TS3 being purchased in large numbers.
*BaMMOT collection*

# Historical Background

The Birmingham & Midland Motor Omnibus Co Ltd (BMMO) was registered on 26 November 1904, but at this time it was merely an attempt by the Birmingham Motor Express Co Ltd — a private company formed in 1903 — to widen its scope by floating a new company. The shares were to be available to the general public but, unfortunately, little interest was shown. As a result, on 5 June 1905, all the directors but one resigned, being replaced by nominees of the British Electric Traction Co Ltd, who had agreed to provide the necessary funds to enable the new company to carry out its plans.

BET had from 27 September 1899 been operating the horse omnibus undertaking of the bankrupt Birmingham General Omnibus Co, an amalgamation of a number of independent operators 'to effect a monopoly of the omnibus system in Birmingham' — the assets of which had been purchased from the Official Receiver. It was this company that had decided, when ordering new buses in March 1900, to have them painted red, and on 1 January 1902 its operations were placed under the control of the Birmingham & Midland Tramways Ltd. Thus the name Midland Red was coined.

From 1 June 1905, therefore, the BMMO Company officially took over the 15 double-deck motor omnibuses formerly operated by the Birmingham Motor Express Co on the Hagley Road and Harborne routes, as well as some 100 horse omnibuses and 1,000 horses previously worked by the City of Birmingham Tramways Co Ltd and the Birmingham & Midland Tramways Ltd in various parts of the city. There were also four additional motor omnibuses which the CBT had put into service on the Harborne routes to compete with the BME.

The maintenance of the motor vehicles proved a continual problem and on 5 October 1907 they were all withdrawn from service and horsebuses restored in their place. However, the BMMO Company found that the horse omnibuses were quite unable to compete with the new electric tramcars and as each new corporation tramway route was opened, the corresponding horsebus service was withdrawn. In any case, it was a condition of the licence issued by the Birmingham Watch Committee at that time that omnibuses should not run on tramway routes. Thus, by 1911 the company's operations were confined almost entirely to the Hagley Road and Harborne routes, where there were no tramways. BMMO reintroduced

motorbuses in 1912 and having inspected a number of models opted for the Tilling-Stevens petrol-electric chassis as the absence of gears made it easier for a horsebus driver to learn the controls! This time around the motorbus was a much greater success. All the existing horsebus routes were speedily converted to motor traction and during 1913 local routes were opened up in Smethwick, Oldbury and Sutton Coldfield.

It is worth noting at this point the rather unorthodox, but successful, management structure at BMMO. In charge of BMMO traffic matters from the inception of the company's operations was Mr O. C. Power, and from 1912 engineering was the responsibility of Mr L. G. Wyndham Shire. For nearly 40 years BMMO had no General Manager, the Engineering and Traffic Departments being controlled independently by these two great personalities who seldom saw eye to eye! An interesting by-product of this separation of interests was that drivers were under the aegis of Mr Shire and conductors under Mr Power, each with quite different uniforms of brown and blue respectively!

▲ Six 1904 Milnes-Daimlers with Milnes Car Company 36 seat bodywork passed from the Birmingham Express Company to BMMO with the Hagley Road route in 1905. None of the vehicles were in very good condition and breakdowns were frequent! One of the six, (O 266), photographed in Sandon Road, Bearwood was withdrawn in 1906 and scrapped in 1907. *BaMMOT collection*

In September 1913 the Birmingham Corporation tramway along the Hagley Road was opened and, in accordance with the Watch Committee's ruling, Midland Red buses were no longer able to use this thoroughfare. It was now plain that the chances of the BMMO Co being able to extend its services inside the city would be extremely limited. The corporation also thought it would be a good plan to have both tramway and motor omnibus services under one control and negotiations were entered into, culminating in an agreement dated 14 February 1914 whereby the corporation was to purchase from the company the leasehold interest in the Tennant Street garage together with 30 Tilling-Stevens double-deck buses then licensed to ply for hire in Birmingham. The

company was not to compete with the corporation inside the city, but was permitted to run through services of motor omnibuses between the centre of Birmingham and places outside the city over the tram routes, as long as suitable protection was given to the services of the corporation, who in turn were not to compete with the company outside the city.

The BMMO Co moved its headquarters to Bearwood and lost no time in opening up its new sphere of operations. The first service was from Birmingham to Walsall in 1913 and this was followed in 1914 with services from Birmingham to Coventry, Stourbridge, Redditch, Kidderminster, Stratford-upon-Avon, Great Malvern and Evesham. The war impeded the company's development but once the war was over, it was

The first company-built chassis was the Standard SOS. This was a 32-seat normal control single-decker, based on the Tilling-Stevens TS3 but with a more reliable gearbox and plate clutch transmission. Early chassis frames were actually built by Tilling's. The engine was based on the Tilling design but with Ricardo alloy cylinder heads and alloy pistons giving a high revving performance with plenty of power from the 4-cylinder SOS petrol engine. Bodywork came from Brush, Carlyle and Ransomes whilst 17 chassis received Davidson charabanc bodies. A marvellous period shot shows (HA 2491), a 1925 example with Ransomes bodywork, in Ashby-de-la-Zouch on 12 May 1934, its last year of service.
*S. L. Smith*

able to set about an expansion programme. In 1919 a number of new routes were opened from a garage in Banbury and the BET tramway depot at Sedgley was used as a base for new operations in the Black Country until a larger garage was opened at Wolverhampton the following year.

Agreements defining areas of operation were drawn up with the Corporation of Walsall in 1919, and with Wolverhampton and Coventry in 1920. Also in 1920, Midland Red vehicles were first domiciled at Hereford and Bromsgrove, and the following year at Leamington, Coventry and Stafford. Although Leicester was destined to become one of the company's largest and most prosperous areas of operation, a garage there had to wait until 1922.

The years after the war were a period of intense competition but the BMMO Co had decided upon a policy of attack and no mileage was curtailed so long as a reasonable return could be obtained. However, it was found that the Tilling-Stevens petrol-electric bus was somewhat outmatched by the small vehicles commonly used by the opposition and, after experiments with similar vehicles, Mr Wyndham Shire came to the conclusion that what was required was something combining the lightness of the small vehicles with the capacity

of the Tilling-Stevens. From 1923 to 1970, therefore, the BMMO Co designed and built most of its own vehicles specifically for the work they had to do. From 1923 to 1940 the initials 'SOS' were used to identify the company's chassis output and much speculation exists as to what the initials stood for. Two interpretations are often mooted — 'Shire's Omnibus Specification' and 'Superior Omnibus Specification' — but it has not been possible to totally verify either version, although there is evidence to support the latter. When production recommenced after the war, until the final output in 1970, all company-built vehicles were badged 'BMMO'.

Although BMMO had deliberately refrained from competing with the BET tramways in the Black Country, this left the door open for other operators to abstract the tram traffic. From 1924 the company was called upon to operate over the tramway routes and create stiff competition for the opposition. From 1926 onwards the various tramways were gradually abandoned in favour of Midland Red buses, which consequently required more garages to be opened. Further operating agreements were entered into with the local authorities of Dudley in 1929, West Bromwich in 1930, and Smethwick, Oldbury, Rowley Regis and Tipton in 1939.

At Worcester, the BET-owned tramways were acquired by Worcester Corporation and, instead of operating its own buses, an agreement was entered into whereby BMMO operated all the city services on behalf of the corporation, paying to it the net profits on all routes passing through the city on a proportionate route mileage basis for that portion of the route within the city. The agreement came into force on 1 June 1928, and then became the basis of most other agreements between the company and other local authorities.

In April 1930 half of the ordinary shares of the BMMO Co were purchased jointly by the Great Western Railway and the London, Midland & Scottish Railway, thus reflecting a period when each of the big four railway companies were busily engaged in acquiring interests in the major bus companies. Also in April 1930, BMMO purchased the undertaking of Black & White Motorways Ltd, of Cheltenham, one of the principal operators of long-distance coach services. Black & White retained its separate identity, however, and the control was shared with two other companies. BMMO had itself been operating long-distance services from Birmingham to coastal resorts since 1921 and extended tours had begun in 1927.

Prior to 1930, omnibus licences were only issued by those local authorities who cared to adopt the necessary powers, and in most places, therefore, no licence of any kind was required. Consequently, BMMO was not in the habit of purchasing established businesses, for it was simpler to start up a service in direct competition with an existing operator rather than spend money on a purchase, with no guarantee that there would not be further opposition from yet another operator the next day. Nevertheless, many services were pioneered by BMMO itself and, as the company continued to expand, it was found necessary to open new garages at Coalville in 1925, at Rugby and Wellington (Salop) in 1926, at Malvern and in the centre of Birmingham (at Digbeth) in 1929.

The effect of the Road Traffic Act (1930) was to bring the bus industry under the close control of area Traffic Commissioners who, in granting 'road service licences', had to take into consideration any representations by persons already providing transport facilities along or near a proposed route. A licence now assumed a cash value and a small operator could command a fair price for its goodwill. Between 1931 and 1939 more than 150 small businesses were purchased by BMMO to fill gaps in its system, the most important being those of the Red House Garage Co Ltd of Coventry, the Leicester & District Bus Co in 1936, Messrs G. H. Burnham of Clifton-on-Teme and P. Owen & Sons Ltd of Abberley in 1938. Contrary to normal practice, BMMO actually took over and operated some of the Leicester & District Albion vehicles, still in their green livery, with 'Midland' fleetname. BMMO was, however, not averse to disposing of its own loss making services if somebody else could be found to operate them more economically and a number of market services in Herefordshire were taken over by the Yeomans family in 1934.

With the extra vehicles required to operate the additional services taken over, the BMMO fleet had now passed the thousand mark and further garage accommodation was necessary at Evesham, Redditch and Swadlincote in 1931, Sutton Coldfield in 1934, Hinckley in 1935, and a second garage in Leicester in 1937. When in 1935 the BMMO Co bought the whole of the issued share capital of the Leamington & Warwick Transport Co, part of the agreement included the purchase of the Stratford-upon-Avon Blue Motors Ltd, with whom BMMO had had a working agreement since 1932. The Stratford company continued to operate as a separate subsidiary

In 1929, 51 Standard SOSs were rebodied with attractive United (Eastern Counties) 26-seat bodies and classified SOS ODD. Whilst regarded as conversions they were virtually new vehicles although the mechanical specification remained identical to the Standard SOS. *BaMMOT collection*

A shot taken in Shrewsbury garage on 9 August 1935 shows the racks of destination boards that were placed on the front and rear of vehicles prior to the introduction of destination blinds. *BaMMOT collection*

until finally absorbed in 1971. Somewhat surprisingly, BMMO did not supply a fleet of vehicles of its own manufacture and, under BMMO control, the Stratford fleet was made up mostly of second-hand Tilling-Stevens vehicles until 1947, when new Leyland vehicles became standard.

The outbreak of war in 1939 meant fuel rationing, the suspension of some services and reduced frequencies on others, a complete halt to long-distance coach services and, of course, no tours or excursions of any kind. A number of vehicles were commandeered while parts of certain garages were requisitioned for the war effort. The production of the company's vehicles at Carlyle Road had to stop, and, excluding notable experimental prototypes, the only new vehicles added to the fleet during the war were 106 double-deckers of 'outside' manufacture, allocated to the company by the Ministry of Supply.

The war years also brought big changes in the management of the company. In April 1940 Mr Wyndham Shire retired and was replaced as Chief Engineer by Mr D. M. Sinclair who had been Assistant Chief Engineer of the Northern General Transport Co Ltd. In October 1943 the Traffic Manager, Mr O. C. Power, died suddenly, and shortly afterwards Mr Sinclair was appointed the company's first General Manager. So ended the unusual arrangement which had overseen BMMO's expansion to become England's largest bus company. In engineering matters, Mr Sinclair's ideas were to prove just as advanced as those of his predecessor. The BMMO Co was the first to adopt wholeheartedly the underfloor engine layout and must be responsible for its subsequent popularity until the arrival of the rear-engined designs — a layout which had been pioneered by Mr Shire in 1935 and subsequently abandoned as unsatisfactory!

The early postwar years saw the reintroduction of vehicle production at Carlyle Road and the restoration of many facilities that had been curtailed, whilst the travel boom and new housing estates created a demand for increased frequencies and new services. Where possible, double-deck vehicles were introduced and a major programme of building and extending garages was undertaken to cater for an increased fleet. However, the good times were not to last. Costs such as wages and fuel were continuing to rise and the company found it necessary to raise fares on a regular basis. The BMMO Co reached its zenith between 1955 and 1956 when passengers-carried figures got very close to 500 million per annum. From then on passenger figures began to drop as more and more people were able to afford private motoring, whilst the impact of television slashed evening leisure traffic.

The company had suffered from an ever worsening staff shortage since the war, and as one way of trying to alleviate this, one-man operation of single-deck vehicles was introduced in 1956. The expansion of one-man operation by Midland Red was for some years quite slow, in many cases involving protracted and tedious negotiation, but it gradually spread throughout the system.

Mr Sinclair retired at the end of 1966 and he was succeeded by his deputy, Mr J. W. Womar, who had been General Manager of the Potteries Motor Traction Ltd. Despite the openly declared opposition by the company to the nationalisation of transport, it was announced in November 1967 that the state-owned Transport Holding Co had acquired the shareholdings of the British Electric Traction Co Ltd. Thus, from March 1968 Midland Red became wholly owned by the Transport Holding Co and in due course, on 1 January 1969, became a subsidiary of the new National Bus Co, set up by the Transport Act (1968).

The SOS FS of 1926, not to be confused with the earlier Tilling-Stevens double-deckers of the same designation, was a logical development of the Standard SOS built to the same basic mechanical specification but with a forward control layout allowing 34 seats in the body space. The 18 charabanc examples, all bodied again by Davidson, were very attractive in appearance as shown by (HA 3525). These were all rebuilt into OD class buses in 1929. *Omnibus Society - both pictures*

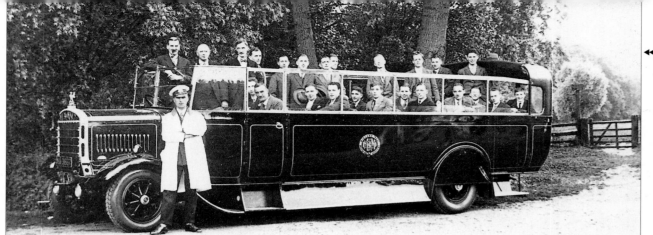

Staff shortages continued on the traffic side and by the late 1960s staffing problems had spread to the engineering section, particularly among the craftsmen who had grown up with the company and were now of retiring age. This led to a gradual rundown in the production of BMMO-built vehicles and the last to be completed entirely at Carlyle Road left the works on 5 January 1970. However, there were still some unfinished vehicles and the bodywork on these was completed by Plaxtons, the last one entering service in June 1970.

It was indeed ironic that the busy car factories that had given Midland Red plenty of business carrying their workers were also, in effect, beginning to undermine the company in two ways. Shortages of bus staff caused by tempting wages in the car industry led to unreliability of service and, at the same time, more cars were being put on the road, tempting passengers away from the buses.

During National Bus Co ownership, economics meant that operations were slimmed considerably. The biggest contraction came with the sale to the West Midlands Passenger Transport Executive of all services operating entirely within the new West Midlands County. Under the Transport Act (1968), the PTE was required to co-ordinate all bus and rail services within its area and this was the only way the two undertakings could meet that objective. Accordingly, on 3 December 1973 413 vehicles, six garages and a large number of staff were transferred to WMPTE. The loss of the Birmingham operations was acknowledged when in March 1974 the official title was changed to the Midland Red Omnibus Co Ltd.

The company was left with an operating territory with a distinctly rural emphasis. Unfortunately, support for rural services rested with county councils whose attitudes to public transport varied widely. In the meantime the £3.6 million received from the West Midlands operations was earmarked for investment to give the company a stronger base for the future, rather than for the short-term expedient of subsidising existing operations. However, although decisions relating to corporate identity, vehicle design and purchasing were naturally influenced by NBC policy, there still existed the innovative spirit in the company which resulted in pioneering work in marketing and computerisation.

A significant development by the company was the Market Analysis Project — originally known as the Viable Network Project. The principle of MAP was that each garage should be able to support itself financially, with the network being slimmed until break-even was achieved. Routes were revised to meet the needs of as many passengers as possible. County councils, of course, were given the opportunity to add to this basic network by providing the necessary financial support. By 1981 the whole of the Midland Red system had received the attention of the MAP men and had been divided into handy compartments, and thus it was not a complete surprise when the announcement came in February 1981 that the company was to be divided into five separate units. In consequence, the Midland Red Omnibus Co Ltd ceased to be an operating company after service on 5 September 1981 and the end of a glorious and significant era had been reached.

◀◀ A unique photograph that only came to light relatively recently shows a splendid publicity shot of (HA 3531) a non-standard FS, basically having a longer wheel base with a short cab. Built in 1926 and thought to have been a Queen type prototype but retaining 34, rather than 37-seat accommodation. It was one of two used when new to promote sales of SOS buses to other operators, the pair being called 'Quantity' and 'Quality'. *BaMMOT collection*

◀ The 14 members of the SOS QC class were the first proper touring coaches designed for the company's use. Although to the same mechanical specification as the Q type, they were of normal control configuration. The 30-seat Carlyle bodywork was a major improvement over previous designs with a single door at the front and a central gangway. Driver Harry Trigg proudly poses with (HA 3667) at Lower Lode, Tewkesbury. *E. V. Trigg/ BaMMOT collection*

## Explanation of SOS Chassis Codes

**SOS S** — Standard SOS was always the official Company designation for this class. The present day abbreviation S type probably originated in the 1940s and is an unofficial term.

**SOS OD** — The names Old Decker and Open-top Development have been suggested as the interpretation of OD. It is not known which, if either, is correct.

**SOS ODD** — The accurate meaning of ODD is not known. The accepted version, OD Development, seems inappropriate but it is possible that ODD was chosen because the only other BMMO conversion had been the OD, a few months earlier. It has also been suggested that the abbreviation means Original Design Development.

**SOS FS** — Two names have been recorded for this class; Forward Steering and Future Standard. It is not known which is correct.

**SOS Q** — Queen. Two buses were used for sales promotional purposes in 1926/7. The pair being publicised as 'Quality and Quantity'. In more recent times both names have been incorrectly quoted as the title for the SOS 'Q' family. The original name is that shown.

**SOS QC** — Queen Charabanc.

**SOS QL** — Queen Low.

**SOS QLC** — Queen Low Charabanc.

**SOS M** — Madam.

**SOS XL** — EXceL. Also recorded as Excelsior. It is not known which is correct.

**SOS MM** — Modified Madam. Also recorded as Modern(ised) Madam. It is not known which is correct.

**SOS COD** — Clarke's Own Design or Clarke's Omnibus Design. The authenticity of either type name cannot be confirmed.

**SOS RR** — Rolls-Royce.

**SOS IM** — Improved Madam. Was redesignated IM4 by circa 1934.

**SOS IM4D** — Improved Madam 4 (cylinder) Development.

**SOS IM6** — Improved Madam 6 (cylinder).

**SOS SRR** — Short (Brothers) Rolls-Royce.

**SOS DD (RE)** — Double Decker (Rear Entrance). The original designation for this class was DD. In 1934 it was officially changed to DD (RE) upon the quantity introduction of front-entrance double-deckers. By circa 1942 the class was generally being quoted as the REDD type.

**SOS BRR** — Bus Rolls-Royce.

**SOS LRR** — Low Rolls-Royce.

**SOS ON/CON/DON** — Onward, Converted Onward, and Diesel Onward.

**SOS OLR** — Open Low Rolls-Royce.

**SOS FEDD** — Front Entrance Double Decker. Class originally designated DD(FE). By 1936 identified as FEDD to avoid confusion with the DD (RE) type.

**SOS SLR** — Saloon Low Rolls-Royce.

**SOS REC** — Rear Engined Coach.

**SOS SON** — Saloon Onward.

**SOS ONC** — Onward Coach.

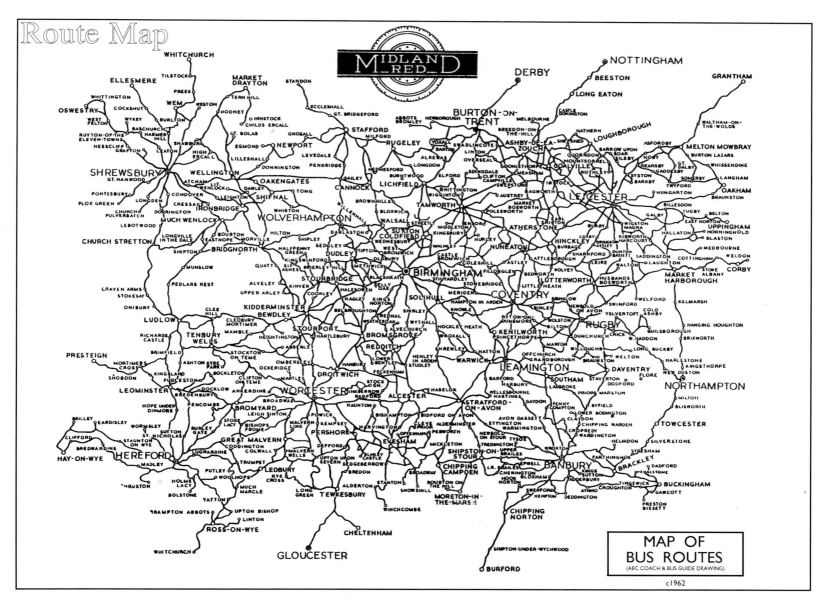

MAP OF
BUS ROUTES
(ABC COACH & BUS GUIDE DRAWING)

c1962

13

The SOS Q arose from a desire to design a maximum capacity single-deck within the overall dimensions of the FS type. They were 37 seaters and with an unladen weight of 4ton 4cwt 2qtr were amongst the lightest full size buses ever built. To achieve the maximum capacity the bulkhead was moved as far forward as possible and to compensate for the driver's restricted area the engine, bonnet and radiator were moved off-centre towards the nearside. This arrangement became standard on all future SOS half-cab designs. (HA 3608) awaits its next duty at The Newarke in Leicester.
*Mike Greenwood collection*

A Brush-bodied Q prepares to pass a rather more rudimentary form of transport in Ansty village whilst working the Leicester to Coventry service.
*Arnold Stringer/Tom Moore collection*

Midland Red utilised a number of their redundant buses in a service vehicle capacity.
Q type (HA 3653) is seen at work under the Warwick Station bridge on 6 August 1937. *Ian Allan Library*

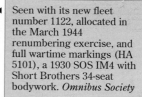

◄ Seen with its new fleet number 1122, allocated in the March 1944 renumbering exercise, and full wartime markings (HA 5101), a 1930 SOS IM4 with Short Brothers 34-seat bodywork. *Omnibus Society*

▼ Another IM4, but of 1932 manufacture with Brush bodywork, was (HA 8286). *Omnibus Society*

In comparison with the photograph (*right*), (HA 8048) shows how the Metro-Cammell bodied REDDs looked on delivery. (HA 8048) was photographed at The Newarke, Leicester in August 1933. *G. H. F. Atkins*

Midland. Red. Mystery. Trip. 1932.  3.

One of the most amazing finds was the discovery of (HA 8047) a SOS REDD in 1994. It was one of the first batch of 50 double-deckers with Midland Red's own chassis. (HA 8047) was built in 1933 with Metro-Cammell 52-seat bodywork and was not withdrawn until 1951.  It apparently then spent most, if not all, of the next 43 years in a wood in Gloucestershire before being rescued by the Oxford Bus Museum.
*Alan King/BaMMOT collection*

Did they ever get back? A rather apprehensive group of people about to embark on a mystery trip in 1932! Their steed was a new Brush-bodied SOS IM4.
*BaMMOT collection*

From the same batch of vehicles was (HA 8249) which, when photographed, was looking somewhat shabby. The lack of an 'A' fleet number and the wartime markings would indicate that the photograph was taken in the early 1940s. (HA 8249) was eventually renumbered 1322 and withdrawn in 1950.
*Omnibus Society*

In 1934 the SOS ON was introduced to take advantage of the then maximum length of 27ft 6in for two axle single-deckers. The increased length and short-bonneted, compact engine allowed no less than 38 seats. In 1937/8 a total of 44 ONs were fitted with BMMO 8 litre K type diesel engines and reclassified CON (Converted ON). A body rebuilding programme took place between 1946 and 1952. No 1503 had its body rebuilt by Nudd Brothers in 1949 and it lasted in this form until withdrawal in 1957.
*Phil Norris Collection - both pictures*

By 1935 a new fleet of touring coaches was required to replace certain of the QLC type. The vehicle developed to meet this requirement was the SOS OLR. The batch had Short Brothers 29-seat bodies and looked dated even when new! They were the last open coaches and the last normal control chassis produced by the Company. The class was demoted to bus duty during the war which included extensive rebuilding to forward control and the fitting of a fixed roof. (AHA 612) is seen when new on the 20 July 1935. *BaMMOT collection*

Former Midland Red buses were very popular with showmen and large numbers of vehicles had their lives extended in this capacity. SOS IM6 (HA 8323) is seen at the Nottingham Goose Fair in October 1958. *G. H. F. Atkins*

The LRR class had originally been built as 30-seat coaches in 1933-1935 but during the war they were converted to 34-seat buses. (AHA 587) was withdrawn in 1952 and by October of the same year was being used by a showman at the Nottingham Goose Fair. *G. H. F. Atkins*

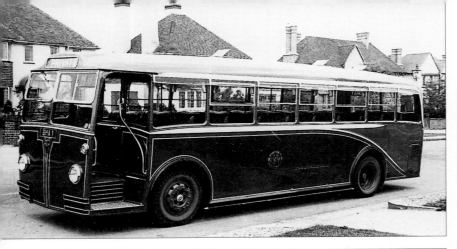

Four REC types were built in 1935/6 and were best known by their registration numbers BHA 1 and CHA 1-3. These vehicles highlighted the technical brilliance, foresight and inventiveness of Mr Shire and pre-dated the design of the modern bus by a quarter of a century! The design was one of the first to feature the driver sitting ahead of the front axle commanding a view of the front entrance. The revolutionary chassis had a petrol engine positioned transversely at the rear of the frame, behind the rear axle, and two radiators, one on each side of the vehicle. A two-pedal control arrangement was provided. The bodywork was constructed by Carlyle Works. All four REC's operated until the war when they were dismantled, some parts being used in wartime building. A fault that they constantly suffered from was the ingress of dirt into the engine but, had history been different, large fleets of these vehicles might have been seen in the 1940s. *BaMMOT collection*

The SOS FEDD echoed the layout of the Tilling-Stevens FS double-deckers of a decade earlier. As the company only operated forward-entrance single-deckers, it seemed obvious to introduce a modern forward-entrance double-decker. Including the prototype, 336 models were built over the period 1933-9 although interestingly 337 bodies were built! An extra FEDD body was built in 1936 (the only one supplied by English Electric) and fitted to a 1934 chassis. In consequence, the Company always had a spare body for the 1934-6 FEDD chassis until 1949, when a Short Brothers body was scrapped. (BHA 344) was one of 135 Metro-Cammell-bodied vehicles delivered in 1935/6. The 56-seat bodywork was exceptionally good and remained in original condition throughout nearly 20 years service. *Omnibus Society*

No 1774 (BHA 329), a 1936 delivery, clearly demonstrates the quality of the bodywork with no noticeable sag despite 19 years of rigorous service. Laying over at St Margaret's, Leicester in August 1955 this bus was withdrawn the following year and became a builder's shed at Walsgrave, Coventry! *G. H. F. Atkins*

The next batch of 50 buses appeared in 1938 to a new design. The composite 56-seat bodywork by Brush had a new outline with single folding 'jack-knife' door in a recessed entrance replacing the sliding door of the previous versions. The new outline included a stepped edge below the windscreen. Tradition was broken on this batch as the fuel tank was moved from its usual position (for SOS) under the driver's seat, to the offside front of the chassis frame. A new radiator was introduced on four of the batch bearing some resemblance to the well known AEC style and the rest of the batch were eventually similarly converted. Two views show the same bus 2135 (EHA 267). The upper photograph was taken at St Margaret's Bus Station, Leicester on 28 September 1956 whilst the lower off-side photograph, taken on a cold, damp day in February 1958, clearly shows the repositioned fuel tank. Western Boulevard, Leicester is the location on this occasion. No 2135 was to last until 1960 before being withdrawn from service.
*Richard Butler - both pictures*

A further batch of 50 Brush-bodied buses was delivered in 1938/39. They were similar to the previous batch except that the fuel tank reverted to beneath the driver's seat. (FHA 218) is seen helping to move the massive queues on the very popular 144 service from Birmingham to Worcester and the Malverns. *R. Norton*

(FHA 840) came from the final batch of 50 FEDD buses delivered in 1939 and clearly shows the fuel tank back under the driver's seat! No 2336 is seen in Birmingham Bull Ring *c*1950. *G. H. F. Atkins*

All Midland Red built postwar double-deckers featured concealed radiators, just one example of the company leading in the field of vehicle design. Some will correctly argue that visibility to the nearside was hampered and engine removal restricted but the streamlining effect of concealing the radiator is indisputable. SOS FEDD (EHA 299) was, however, the prototype being rebuilt to this form in October 1942. The bus is seen in Walsall just prior to being returned to conventional layout in 1951. *Tom Moore collection*

A fine shot of No 2347 (FHA 851) working the 'Track', the Birmingham to Dudley group of services, late in its life. *Robert Hannay*

'Mind how you go' was the advice offered to waiting passengers at the Worcester Agricultural Show in June 1949! Two 1937 30-seat English Electric-bodied SOS SLRs stand ready for loading. Part of a batch of 50 vehicles, they were mechanically similar to the 1935 OLR models but of forward control configuration. *BaMMOT collection*

SOS SLR (CHA 979), in original condition, is attempting to attract customers for an evening tour to Church Eaton at a cost of only two shillings return. It rather begs the question of whether the return trip was compulsory! *Omnibus Society*

In comparison to the picture (*above right*) SLR (CHA 965) shows the simplified mouldings and new grille received in the postwar years. No 1983 was withdrawn from service in 1955 and became a dual-control training vehicle. *Peter Yeomans*

Between 1935 and 1940 the SOS SON was built in large numbers, a total of 330 vehicles being produced including a small batch for the Trent Motor Traction Company. They were fitted with the 8 litre 'K' type oil engine as well as the standard 'Silent 3rd' gearboxes. No 2298 (FHA 453) entered service as part of a batch of thirty-eight vehicles in 1939 and they were the first single-deckers with the new shape radiator. Original bodywork was by Brush but by the time that No 2298 was photographed at Nuneaton in October 1955 it had been rebuilt by Nudd Brothers.
*G. H. F. Atkins*

1939 example (FHA 483) lies idle amongst late 1940s and mid 1950s BMMO models at Leicester. No 2328, another Nudd Brothers rebuild, was withdrawn from service in 1957.
*Mike Greenwood collection*

The last SOSs built for the Company's use were 50 Brush-bodied SON 38-seaters delivered in 1940 and registered (GHA 301-350). The body style was similar to the previous batch but more rounded at the front and rear. No 2421 (GHA 340), from the final batch of SONs, loads in Burton upon Trent bus station. A new improved type of seating was fitted and for the first time used ticket boxes were provided. Rebuilding, in No 2421's case again by Nudd Brothers, did little harm to the smooth lines of the GHA SONs. The last 14 SOS chassis, which immediately followed the GHA-series for BMMO, were supplied to Trent to become that Company's Nos 412-425 (RC 7922-35). Happily No 417 survived into preservation and has been immaculately restored by the Company, whilst BMMO No 2418 (GHA 337) is preserved at the Transport Museum, Wythall. *Peter Yeomans*

▶ An unusual vantage point finds No 2390 (GHA 309) on its way to Coalville on 21 May 1956, another of the class that was rebuilt by Nudd Brothers in 1951. The short bonnet of the SON emphasises how compact the Kidney engine was. No other 6-cylinder unit of comparable size would fit in these vehicles, yet the BMMO product compared well with engines built by other UK manufacturers. It was efficient, smooth-running and very reliable. *Richard Butler*

▲ The 25 ONC coaches with Duple 30-seat centre-entrance bodies were the first SOS coaches built new with diesel engines. The BMMO K type 8-litre oil engine drove through an Aphon gearbox with overdrive giving a most satisfactory degree of refinement. Refined enough obviously for a visiting Australian touring cricket team! Looking somewhat bemused, team members and officials pose in front of an unidentified member of the class. Note the young Richie Benaud in the middle of the group. *BaMMOT collection*

◀ In 1958 Mr P Garrow-Fisher purchased three ONCs from Midland Red for use on a London-Bombay-London tour and all were appropriately lettered at Carlyle Works. Did they ever make it? Did they get back? Where are they now? *G H Stone*

Delivered in 1939, the ONC class comprised the last SOS coach design and introduced a red and black coach livery to the fleet. No 2287 (FHA 419) basks in the sunshine with another member of the class and three BMMO service buses. The ONC class provided sterling service not being withdrawn until the period 1958-1960. No 2286, however, enjoyed an extended life. Having a sliding roof it was ideal for football teams to tour cities and greet their fans after important matches. It was used, as required, in this capacity until 1963 by then some 24 years old!
*Mike Greenwood collection*

BMMO production stopped during the war and the Company received a variety of AEC, Daimler, Guy and Leyland double-deckers allocated by the Ministry of War Transport. Three Northern Counties-bodied Leyland Titan TD7s bore little resemblance to most of the austere buses then entering service around the country. The Ministry of Supply granted a dispensation to Northern Counties allowing them to build in metal, because the Company had few facilities for making wood framing and also had a stock of material for metal framed bodies. Thus the builder's products were built to a more relaxed specification than those produced elsewhere. No 2439 (GHA 793) was delivered in 1942, and withdrawn in 1955.
*The late Don Morris/Tom Moore collection*

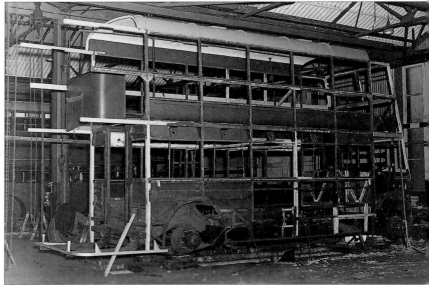

Eight 56-seat Daimler CWA6s with Brush bodies were delivered in 1945. Numbered 2542-49 (GHA 992-999) these, like all the wartime utility vehicles, went through a programme of body rebuilding in the early 1950s. Seven of the eight were dealt with by Willowbrook at its Loughborough works in 1951, whilst No 2546 was the prototype Daimler rebuild carried out by Carlyle in 1949. (*Above*) shows No 2547 in original condition, whilst the extent of the rebuild can be judged by the (*Below Left*) picture. Finally the finished product, this time in the shape of No 2542 is shown (*Above Right*).
*Brian Dicks collection*

(CHA 1), the former SOS REC coach, was reconstructed in 1942. Its original body was sold, being considered unsuitable for conversion. Instead, the body from (CHA 2) was rebuilt to a style which evolved into the postwar single-deckers. By this time Mr Donald Sinclair had taken the place of Mr Shire, who had retired in 1940. Mr Sinclair was convinced that the amidships, underfloor engine was the pattern for the future and this was the principle adopted on the appropriately numbered No 1942 (CHA 1). In 1945 a new model identification numbering system was introduced with single-deckers designated S, coaches C and double-deckers D. Thus (CHA 1) became an S2, with (BHA 1) being the S1. No 1942 lasted in the form illustrated until withdrawal in 1957. *Mike Greenwood collection*

During the closing stages of the war a new double-deck, of revolutionary styling, appeared. Registered (HHA 1), it had a Weymann 56-seat four bay body of all-metal construction with a rear entrance. For a vehicle produced in an 'austerity' period its styling was dramatic and was to influence postwar double-deck design nationally. Although the body was built by Weymann the design was pure Midland Red. The chassis followed the specification for the prewar FEDD with a K type 8.028 litre oil engine but improved by flexible engine mountings. (HHA 1) received the designation D1 and fleet number 2541. *Omnibus Society*

In 1949 platform doors were fitted to the D1 prior to their adoption on all new BMMO double-deckers. An emergency door at the rear, clearly shown here, was fitted to comply with regulations. Based at Bearwood garage throughout its life, No 2541 was not withdrawn until 1961. *Ian Allan library*

Carlyle Road Works at Edgbaston, Birmingham or Central Works (as it became known) was a vastly important site for the Company. Its responsibilities went far beyond those normally associated with a bus overhaul and repair unit and its achievements grew to a prominence that has rarely been equalled in the industry. During the First World War the site was partially occupied by the Royal Flying Corps, although it was owned by the Daimler Company and used for the manufacture of aircraft. In 1920 a substantial part of the property was purchased by BMMO and in 1924 the remaining area was acquired. From early in 1925 new chassis were assembled on the site, the work having previously been undertaken at Bearwood garage. The site was developed on a number of occasions and it is believed that the photograph illustrated here shows the final major redevelopment of 1954. The last BMMO produced buses came off the production line here in 1970. *BaMMOT collection*

No 2579 (HHA 222) was the first completely new underfloor-engined single-decker. Designated S5 it entered service in 1946. The vehicle was of integral construction, the 40-seat bodywork being built by Metro Cammell. *BaMMOT collection (both photographs)*

The batch of 100 S6 single-deckers delivered in late 1946 and during 1947, represented the fruition of wartime development work. They started a new fleet number series, 3000-99 and carried registration numbers (HHA 601-700). At the time the registration numbers were booked, the batch was to have been numbered 2601-2700. No 3061 (HHA 662), with 30-seat Brush bodywork, picks up passengers on the outskirts of Birmingham. *Alan Cross*

The early post-war Midland Red double-decker, with its half cab, may have lacked some of the modernity of the contemporary BMMO single-decker but nevertheless was a most striking vehicle. The AEC Regent Mk II chassis of the 100-strong AD2 class was quite the reverse, however, being a well-tried but old fashioned design, that was purchased because BMMO production capacity was fully occupied building single-deckers. No 3111 (JHA 12), with Brush bodywork, is seen at Stourbridge when new. *BaMMOT collection*

# Midland Red Operating Statistics

| Year | Fleet Size | Passengers Carried |
|------|-----------|-------------------|
| 1914 | 53 | 10,954,995 |
| 1924 | 326 | 34,114,000 |
| 1934 | 1045 | 145,882,777 |
| 1944 | 1432 | 327,424,183 |
| 1952 | 1813 | 461,548,816 |
| 1953 | 1811 | 452,269,324 |
| 1954 | 1903 | 457,367,962 |
| 1955 | 1858 | 474,438,057 |
| 1956 | 1879 | 484,120,881 |
| 1957 | 1872 | 375,793,628 |
| 1958 | 1844 | 386,976,988 |
| 1959 | 1870 | 370,713,009 |
| 1960 | 1874 | 370,683,302 |
| 1961 | 1896 | 355,725,299 |
| 1962 | 1897 | 342,930,295 |
| 1963 | 1906 | 342,818,239 |
| 1964 | 1920 | 329,901,662 |
| 1965 | 1869 | 295,952,867 |
| 1966 | 1783 | 276,695,636 |
| 1967 | 1752 | 267,966,593 |
| 1968 | 1718 | 255,133,520 |
| 1969 | 1761 | 235,870,115 |
| 1970 | 1720 | 211,576,952 |
| 1971 | 1655 | 197,577,089 |
| 1972 | 1594 | 189,760,909 |
| 1973 | 1278 | 185,372,009 |
| 1974 | 1305 | 123,434,566 |
| 1975 | 1263 | 113,706,117 |
| 1976 | n/a | 105,799,850 |
| 1977 | 1125 | 102,711,526 |
| 1978 | 1057 | 104,547,082 |
| 1979 | 1004 | 104,083,151 |
| 1980 | 862 | 92,330,502 |

◄ Metro-Cammell-bodied S6, 3038 (HHA 639), stands out of service at St Margaret's Bus Station, Leicester on a spring morning in May 1963. *Chris Aston*

► Midland Red were always keen to encourage leisure traffic and accordingly produced a wide range of suitable publicity along with the value for money 'Day Anywhere' tickets. This also resulted in many enthusiasts travelling many a mile on the Company's buses. Midland Red kept that interest alive by producing regluar pocket fleet lists and photographs of the latest fleet additions.

It was General Manager Donald Sinclair who coined the phrase 'The Friendly Midland Red' and he insisted that the Company lived up to the title! *Mike Greenwood*

Midland Red took advantage of the newly permitted wider dimensions of 8ft 0in with the appropriately named S8. The designation S7 was thus not used. The batch of 100 vehicles all carried Metro-Cammell 40-seat bodies. No 3268 (JHA 868), photographed on 6 June 1965, illustrates the very rural nature of some of Midland Red's routes!
*Malcolm Keeley*

The first postwar Midland Red coaches, delivered in 1948/9, were based on the single-deck service bus chassis and were thus just as technically advanced being years ahead of their time. Fitted with 30-seat centre-entrance Duple bodies, the restrained styling did not date and the majority of the 45 C1 coaches lasted well into the 1960s. Many were still in very good condition and nine were retained by the Company for driving training duties. No 3327 is seen in Victoria Square, Birmingham on 10 August 1973. The instructor must have been confident in the trainee because the nearside front seat with access to the second steering wheel and foot controls was vacant!
*Malcolm Keeley*

Twelve similar C2 coaches followed in 1950. Intended primarily for extended tours they seated only 26. Nine of the class were upseated to 30 upon delivery of new, bigger touring coaches in 1954. A few smaller touring coaches were still required and Nos 3351, 3354 and 3356 remained as 26-seaters until 1959 when they were converted to 30-seaters (although still on coach cruise work) and modernised with new grilles and bumpers. *Geoff Lumb*

The modernised C2s were, however, getting on in years for coach cruise work so Nos 3346, 3350 and 3352 were rigorously overhauled in 1962 and then rebodied with 26-seat Plaxton Embassy bodies, being redesignated CL2. No 3352 is seen in Stratford-upon-Avon in September 1966. All three were withdrawn in 1971. *Mike Sutcliffe*

The production version of the BMMO postwar double-decker appeared in 1949 and was an 8 ft 0 in wide version of the D1 prototype. The power unit was the BMMO 8.028 litre diesel driving through a gearbox in the chassis frame. Bodywork was by Brush with a seating capacity of 56. Designated D5, the batch of 100 vehicles was always highly commended for its quietness and smooth running qualities — thought by some to have been unequalled in the UK postwar bus industry. The type codes between the D1 and D5 were occupied by 100 AD2 class buses (see page 32). While BMMO production capacity was fully occupied building single-deckers the company turned to AEC for the supply of its Regent Mk II chassis. These were bodied in equal numbers by Brush and Metro-Cammell but very much to the Midland Red design. The AD3 were to have been eight RT type Regent IIIs with air operated pre-selective gearboxes and air brakes! Fleet numbers 3300-7 were actually reserved but the order was cancelled and the designation D3 never used. The D4 is something of a mystery and it is thought to have been a prototype chassis that was subsequently abandoned before completion. Early D5 No 3463 is seen in Leicester's St Margaret's Bus Station during March 1964 fitted with a D7 class radiator grille. *Mike Sutcliffe*

D5 No 3508 was an early withdrawal being taken out of service in 1962. It was subsequently converted into a tree-lopper and was photographed in this guise on 22 May 1969. *Malcolm Keeley*

Midland Red was still very short of vehicles in 1949 and thus took delivery of 20 Guy Arab Mk IIIs with Meadows 6DC 630 engines. They were numbered 3557-3576 and classified GD6. The 56-seat bodywork was by Guy on Park Royal frames and was not to BMMO design and looked somewhat dated compared to Midland Red's own sleek styled postwar designs. Later in life they were all re-engined with BMMO K type units. The GD6s were a familiar sight on routes from Dudley garage until their withdrawal in 1961-2. Note the 'Vacancies' advert on No 3562 which became a regular feature during the 1960s.
*Mike Greenwood collection*

Between 1950 and 1952, 100 more Brush-bodied double-deckers were built and numbered 3777-3876 (NHA 777-876). Known as D5Bs, they were fitted with electrically operated four-leaf folding rear entrance doors. These buses led the trend for platform doors. Traditional and superbly constructed, these were the last 'heavy' BMMO-built double-deckers and they were also the last Midland Red double-deckers with Brush bodies. No 3819 works a Leicester local service in June 1966, being withdrawn later in the year.
*Chris Aston*

One hundred Leyland Titan PD2/12s with metal framed Leyland 56-seat bodies were delivered during 1952/53 to supplement production of BMMO-built double-deckers. Virtually standard Leyland bodies were fitted, the most noticeable change being the concealed radiator front-end assembly specified by Midland Red. The new front end became the standard Leyland design for concealed radiator Titans for all operators throughout the remainder of the 1950s and the early 1960s. Designated LD8, No 4022 (SHA 422) is seen in the company of BMMO built D7 No 4464 at St Margaret's Bus Station, Leicester in June 1965. Withdrawals of the LD8 class started in 1965 and the type was eliminated by 1967. *Mike Sutcliffe*

Midland Red's first coach design built to the 30ft 0in x 8ft 0in dimensions was introduced in 1953. Sixty-three C3 chassis received 37-seat Willowbrook bodies and were numbered 4179-4241. In 1962 the company decided to rebody 16 of them. The refurbished chassis were sent to Plaxton's where they received a modified version of the builders Panorama front-entrance body. Seating capacity was 36 and the coaches were designated CL3. No 4237 is seen gleaming in Minehead during June 1965. *Geoff Atkins*

The D7 introduced in 1953 was the first BMMO double-decker built to a lightweight standard. In all 350 were constructed with Metro-Cammell bodies based on the builders newly introduced Orion design. Early examples were 58-seaters but later deliveries had a capacity for 63 passengers. The earlier vehicles were also converted to 63-seaters, except No 4400 which, somehow forgotten, retained its plentiful front upper-deck leg room to the end! Whilst the D7 was mechanically similar to the D5 there were two important changes. The engine and gearbox were mounted together in the chassis frame and the engine was an improved version of the proven BMMO 8.028 litre K type diesel, known as the KL type (Kidney Long). The total vehicle weighed between 7ton 2cwt 0qtr and 7ton 7cwt 1qtr (depending on capacity) and were lively performers. No 4382, from the 1954/5 batch, is seen on the Shrewsbury Garage forecourt.
*Mike Greenwood collection*

A yellow Midland Red bus! No 4130, from the first batch, is seen in Hagley Road, Birmingham on Friday 13 June 1975, perhaps not a good day for learner drivers. Two of the early D7s were withdrawn in 1964 and 1965 and sold to a film studio in the USA. Normal withdrawals commenced in November 1966 and continued until 1972. As well as driver trainers, a number of D7s were cut down and converted to towing vehicles. *Malcolm Keeley*

The 40-seat dual purpose variant of the S14 was introduced in 1957, numbered 4601-50, and designated S15. No 4604 is seen in Nottingham in September 1962 in the attractive red and black livery. Note the small fleet numbers on the off-side corner. *Geoff Atkins*

The prototype S14 appeared in 1954. Chassisless construction was employed, incorporating independent front wheel suspension and toggle link rear suspension with disc brakes on all wheels. Production models first appeared in 1955. The 44-seat body was built to an overall length of 30ft 0in. The most remarkable single achievement was an unladen weight of just over 5 tons. It was possibly the most varied of all BMMO types with over 30 subtle variations recorded in the first batch alone! Production continued until 1959 by which time 219 vehicles had been constructed. No 4716 of the last batch is seen at the Anderson Road/Herbert Road junction, Bearwood in June 1969. *Malcolm Keeley*

No 4706, also from the last batch of S14s, was photographed at Shrewsbury bus station on 30 May 1969. Withdrawal of S14s commenced in 1967 and was completed by 1971. *Geoff Lumb*

The C5 coach was a natural development of the S14/S15 models, sharing their basic integral body framework and mechanical specification but upgraded for coach duties. With glass fibre incorporated wherever possible, including a one-piece moulded roof, the complete vehicle weighed just under 6.5 tons unladen. Ventilation and soundproofing were given a great deal of attention resulting in an extremely pleasant vehicle in which to travel. In November 1959, Britain's first motorway was opened and Midland Red's contribution to the event was the introduction of the first motorway express coach service, between Birmingham and London, with specially built CM5T coaches. The T indicated that the vehicle was fitted with a toilet compartment and consequently a reduced seating capacity of 34 rather than the 37 seats fitted to the other members of the C5 class. Another early variation was the

CM5 which, as the designation implies, was a CM5T without the toilet compartment. When the motorway was first opened there was no mandatory speed limit and the motorway coaches with their turbocharged KL engines regularly ran at speeds of 85mph or more! No 4833 (833 HHA) was converted from a C5 to a CM5 in 1963 for use on the Birmingham to Worcester motorway service. It is seen here loading in Worcester Bus Station for its return trip to Birmingham. *Mike Greenwood collection*

A typical Midland Red wooden timetable case that could be found right across the company's vast empire. This one was photographed at Much Wenlock, Shropshire, on 11 October 1969. *Chris Aston*

As far back as 1951, Midland Red was interested in developing a 30ft 0in long, high capacity double-decker. However, such double-deckers were not legally approved until 1956 at which time Midland Red was successfully developing single-deckers with integral construction, rubber suspension and disc brakes. So, it was not a 30ft 0in D7 which was unveiled in 1958 but instead the prototype of a remarkable and very advanced integral 72-seat machine, the D9. Production vehicles first appeared in 1960 and differed considerably from the prototype, with the fuel tank reverting to the usual off-side position, a more attractive front end, drum brakes and numerous other cosmetic changes. The same basic mechanical specification, however, was retained which included rubber suspension throughout, independently-sprung front wheels, and a new 10.5 litre BMMO KL type engine coupled to an electrically controlled, hydraulically operated, self-changing gear box. Thus, there were only two pedals and gear selection was by a small spring-loaded lever. No 4896 (896 KHA) of the first batch is seen in Broadway *en route* to Evesham.
*Chris Aston*

Production of the D9 continued for six years by which time 345 examples had entered service. Many improvements were made during this time and certain vehicles received special features. In true Midland Red tradition it is debatable whether any two were identical! No 5417 (EHA 417D) of the final 1966 batch, and whose bodywork was completed by Willowbrook, is seen leaving the Bull Ring Bus Station, Birmingham on the 29 March 1973, immaculately outshopped in full NBC poppy red livery.
*Malcolm Keeley*

The share capital of Kemp & Shaw Ltd, Leicester was acquired by Midland Red on 31 July 1955. A fleet of seven Guys and two Leylands was taken over but, as the business continued to be operated as a subsidiary undertaking for the time being, they retained Kemp & Shaw livery. One Guy dating from the wartime years was withdrawn in 1955 but the remaining eight buses passed into the BMMO fleet on 1 January 1959 when Kemp & Shaw was finally liquidated. They subsequently received Midland Red livery and fleet numbers 4838-4845. No 4844 (GRY 763) was a 1950 Leyland PD2/1 with 53-seat low-bridge Leyland bodywork. For many years it looked as though it was going to be the only low-bridge double-decker ever to feature in the BMMO fleet but the entry into service of an ex-PMT low-bridge Leyland Atlantean in 1979 took away this record! No. 4844 is seen at speed in Syston on its way back to Leicester in early evening sunshine during March, 1966. The PD2 had a long career with BMMO, not being withdrawn until 1967. *Chris Aston*

The retention of vehicles acquired with businesses was a very rare event. However, shortly after the total absorption of the Kemp & Shaw fleet, a further three second-hand vehicles were added, upon the takeover of another Leicestershire company. The acquisition of H. Boyer & Son, Rothley on 1st February 1959 added two Sentinels and one Leyland Royal Tiger, all of which were repainted into Midland Red livery. BMMO led the country in introducing underfloor-engined single-deckers after the war but not far behind was the small manufacturing concern of Sentinel — well ahead of the big boys. Sentinels never became very common, most operators waiting until the major builders caught up. It was thus interesting that Midland Red should acquire two examples of the breed. No 4847 (GUT 543), built in 1951, was a late model STC6 with 30ft Sentinel 44-seat body. It was withdrawn by BMMO in 1961. *Peter Smith*

Midland Red in the late 1950s was impressed by the high capacity features of double-deckers being produced by other manufacturers but they did not wish to participate in the fashionable (and unreliable) rear-engined concept. The D9, thought by many to be of almost revolutionary design, was quickly eclipsed by the introduction of the D10, a high capacity under-floor engined, 30ft chassisless double-decker! The design was quite spectacular and again BMMO had achieved something which had eluded the UK bus industry. However, such a design was not without problems, not least accommodating the 10.5 litre BMMO engine below the floor(!), but the skills of the Midland Red designers and engineers managed to overcome all the problems in various novel ways. Sadly only two D10s were ever built, amidst high hopes in the early 1960s that the type would go into full production. Why the design was not perpetuated is not fully understood, but no doubt the changing fortunes of the company, the need for further development and, possibly, influence from outside all played their part! No 4943, together with sister 4944, spent their working lives initially in Birmingham and then based later at Hartshill and Stafford garages. However, they did occassionally venture elsewhere and 4943 (943 KHA) is seen in the company of a D7 at Leicester in March 1964. The D10 was the epitaph of the advanced technology and individuality which were the trademarks of Midland Red engineering, the zenith of achievement which had started with the SOS in 1923. Fortunately, both an SOS Standard and BMMO D10 (No 4943) have been retained for preservation and can be seen at the Transport Museum at Wythall in South Birmingham. *Mike Sutcliffe*

To supplement vehicle production from Carlyle Road Works, Midland Red purchased 100 Leyland Leopard PSU3 buses, the first single-deck vehicles purchased from an outside manufacturer for 40 years! When delivered in 1962/3, they were also the first new vehicles in the fleet for almost 10 years to have separate bodies and chassis. Although to BMMO requirements, the bodywork was to the BET Federation style. No 5180 (5180 HA) was a Willowbrook 48-seat LSl8A example and carried the attractive red and black dual-purpose livery. It is seen leaving Southgate Street Bus Garage, Leicester to take up duty on the 112-mile X91 service to Hereford in May 1963. *Chris Aston*

In 1963 Midland Red received 50 rear-engined Daimler Fleetline CRG6 double-deckers with 77-seat Alexander bodies. Designated DD11, No 5293 (5293 HA) is seen, when new, near Keyham on the rural Hungarton to Leicester service. *Chris Aston*

The success of Midland Red's high-speed motorway services quickly necessitated thoughts of future development. In 1963, a prototype 36ft 0in x 8ft 2½in coach No 5295 (5495 HA) entered service, designated CM6T. It was virtually a lengthened CM5T with the integral construction housing the accepted BMMO specification suitably uprated for motorway duties. Towards the end of 1963 both the interior and exterior were remodelled and it is seen in this form at a rather cold and misty Pool Meadow Bus Station, Coventry. Note that the use of maroon replaced black from 1967 and the 'anti-nationalisation' poster along the roof panels. *Mike Greenwood collection*

In 1962 Midland Red introduced a 52-seat version of the S14 which took advantage of the new legal maximum dimensions for coaches and single-deck buses of 36ft 0in long and 8ft 2½in wide. Designated the S16 they were not totally successful, mainly because they were underpowered and retained an unfashionable manual gearbox making them unpopular with the drivers. In 1963, with performance and ease of operation in mind, the company introduced the S17, a similar vehicle but fitted with a horizontal version of the BMMO 10.5 litre engine and a semi-automatic, two pedal control gearbox. A large number of the vehicles had only the main body structure completed at Carlyle Road Works, being finished by outside contractors, including S17 No 5604 (BHA 604C), seen outside the Willowbrook Coach Works in 1965. *Chris Aston*

Production of the S17 continued until 1966, although rather surprisingly another batch of S16s entered service in 1964 principally to use up stocks of manual gearboxes and BMMO 8 litre KL engines! From the last batch of S17s, Plaxton-finished No 5764 (EHA 764D) is seen in Coventry during August 1975. *Tom Moore*

59

▲

Following the success of the prototype CM6T (see page 57) 29 production vehicles entered service during 1965/6. Between January 1972 and May 1973 the majority of the class entered Carlyle Road Works for overhaul and restyling. The result was an attractive vehicle even in the much decried white National coach livery. Four of the class are seen parked up at the former Harper Brothers Heath Hayes garage on 15 June 1974. *Mike Greenwood*

▶▶ Soon after control of the company had passed to the National Bus Company in 1969, it was announced that vehicle building was to cease. In fairness to NBC, who was blamed for this decision, it should be said that they did not acquire a company in the best of condition and it had major problems needing to be cured. Midland Red had, for some time, suffered a serious staff shortage on both the operating and

engineering sides which, with regard to the latter, had chronically affected maintenance of the fleet and the building of new vehicles. Furthermore, for some years vehicle production had been hopelessly uneconomic and it was also of significance that the NBC had an interest in the Bristol chassis manufacturer and Eastern Coach Works, as the bodybuilder. The final BMMO production programme comprised 76 S23 one-man-operated service buses. They were built between 1968 and 1970 and, whilst similar to preceding classes, changes included the fitting of 51 bus seats and top sliding ventilators in most windows. Bus No 5941 was the last complete BMMO-built vehicle and after a small ceremony at Carlyle Works, it entered service in January 1970. The remaining 50 vehicles had bodywork completed by Plaxton, at Scarborough, including 5962 (UHA 962H) seen here passing S17 5717 (DHA 717C) at Solihull Station on 23 June 1973. *Malcolm Keeley*

The final series of BMMO-built buses was a variation of established principals. All were 36ft 0in long and 8ft 2½in wide and were mechanically almost identical to the S17 type. The body structure was based on the six-bay CM6 production style. Thirty semi-coach S21 type vehicles, designed primarily for light weekday stage carriage work and weekend coach duties, entered service in 1967. Forty-nine blue, very comfortable, high backed seats (with headrests) were fitted and the side windows were fixed with forced ventilation. The class was later demoted to regular stage carriage work as shown in this January 1978 night shot of No 5856 (JHA 856E) in Coventry.
*Tom Moore*

Immediately following the semi-coaches were 37 dual purpose 45-seat buses, designated S22 and delivered in 1968. No 5907 (PHA 507G) loads in Bowling Green Street, Leicester, having been demoted to bus service work by June 1978.
*Mike Greenwood*

A further batch of Daimler Fleetline CRG6s, similar to the DD11 class, was received between 1966 and 1968. Designated DD12, all were converted for one-man operation from 1968 onwards. In 1979 the company celebrated 75 years of operation and to mark the occasion DD12 No 6007 (GHA 407D) was painted into a special livery to recall the earliest days of the company.
*Tom Moore*

Midland Red's choice of coaches from the mid-1960s was the Leyland Leopard in both short and long form. The LC7 class was bodied by Duple, whilst the LC8, LC9 and LC10 classes were all bodied by Plaxton. It was somewhat of a surprise, however, that a batch of 30 PSU3A Leopards delivered in 1970 reverted to the contemporary Panorama design rather than the newer Elite style carried by the 1969 LC10 class. Numbered 6226-6255 (WHA 226-55H), they were coded LC11. No 6228 is seen in Llandudno when new in July 1970.
*Geoff Atkins*

64

In 1969, Midland Red received the first of its second generation Daimler Fleetline double-deckers. They were similar to the 1966-68 deliveries, the principal change being dual entrance/exit configuration. Having said that, it was a very rare occurrence for the centre doors to be used! The class was designated DD13 and No 6262 (YHA 262J) was part of a second batch of DD13s that incorporated a new style lower front-end. It was photographed in Station Road, Solihull on 23 June 1973.
*Malcolm Keeley*

The company decided that the lightweight Ford R192 was the ideal vehicle to replace ageing S14s on rural services. A batch of 100 S25 45-seat Plaxton Derwent-bodied buses was ordered for delivery in 1970/71. Intended to have a seven year life, before sale, it was found necessary to overhaul some of them for extended service, including 6356 (YHA 356J) which loads in Charles Street, Leicester on 14 April 1979. A number of these Fords were later converted for 27-seat midibuses by removing two bays from the bodywork and shortening the chassis. The final major building activity undertaken at Carlyle Works. *Malcolm Keeley*

Despite having a working agreement with Stratford Blue from 1932 it was somewhat surprising that BMMO did not supply a fleet of vehicles of their own manufacture. One SOS SON that did make it into the Stratford Blue fleet, however, was a 1937 example converted into a tree-cutter. Photographed in September 1961, this vehicle was finally withdrawn and scrapped in 1964. *Geoff Lumb*

The Stratford Blue fleet was finally absorbed by Midland Red on 1 January 1971. Forty three mixed Leyland single and double-deck types were numbered in the series 2001-2135 with the majority of vehicles eventually being repainted into Midland Red colours. 1966 Leyland Leopard PSU4 2059 (HAC 628D), with Marshall 41-seat dual purpose bodywork, lasted long enough to receive NBC livery. It was outside Longbridge Works on service 331 in May 1977. *Malcolm Keeley*

Despite the cessation of manufacture of BMMO vehicles, the type classification system continued although the use of an initial letter for 'outside' makes was dropped. In 1971 a large batch of 49-seat Willowbrook bodied dual-purpose S24 class Leyland Leopards was delivered. By the time 6424 (CHA 424K) was photographed it was in NBC dual-purpose livery, albeit the bus was working a Leamington local service. No 5848 (JHA 848E) in the background, was an earlier class LS20 Willowbrook-bodied Leopard. *Tom Moore*

The last Leopards to a purely service bus specification were 13 with Marshall 53-seat bodies received in 1972. No 6470 (DHA 470K), when new in June of that year, leaves Nottingham on the express route to Birmingham. Note that the service was crew operated at the time. This batch also ended the fleet numbering series adopted on vehicles from March 1944 with the highest fleet number used being 6473. *Geoff Atkins*

Fleet numbers reverted back to 101 with the arrival of the initial Leyland National in 1972. The initial batch of 58 vehicles was classified N1. Despite the fact that decisions had been taken on the future livery for vehicles in NBC fleets, No 101 was finished in the normal Midland Red colour scheme as seen here in Broad Street, Birmingham on 31 January 1973. It was the only Leyland National so treated, No 102 and all subsequent vehicles receiving the standard NBC colours from new. *Malcolm Keeley*

More dual-purpose Leyland Leopards arrived in 1973 including No 236 (JHA 236L). This Marshall-bodied S27 class bus loads in Warwick in August 1980 in the company of Leyland National N6 No 602 (NOE 602R) of 1977. *Malcolm Keeley*

Apart from two small batches of Fords, the Leyland National became the mainstay of the bus fleet, although Midland Red's 1975 orders had promised some variety. Along with 25 Nationals, 10 Leopard coaches and 10 Leopard dual-purpose vehicles, the order also called for 40 Bristol LH/ECW service buses and 20 Park Royal-bodied Leyland Atlanteans! In the event the LHs were diverted to Crosville, and 20 Nationals were received in exchange whilst the double-deck order was also changed to Leyland Nationals. No 408 (GOL 408N), a 1975 N3 delivery, takes a good load on board in Rugby during August, 1977. *Tom Moore*

Almost 400 Leyland Nationals were received over the period 1972 to 1979, with No 664 (SOA 664S) being a 1977 N7 example. It was photographed in August 1979 outside one of Warwickshire's more famous landmarks, Anne Hathaway's cottage. *Tom Moore*

In 1973 and 1974, a number of well-established Staffordshire and Shropshire based independents were acquired and in consequence a wide variety of miscellaneous vehicles joined the Midland Red fleet. This included a number of Leyland Titans from the former Harper Brothers fleet, including Northern Counties-bodied PD3A No 2223 (NRF 349F). Repainted into full NBC Midland Red livery, No 2223 passes West Midlands PTE No 4180 in Lower Bull Street, Birmingham on 4 September 1975. Twenty-one months earlier, in December 1973, BMMO bus services which operated wholly within the West Midlands Metropolitan County area had been transferred into the ownership of the West Midlands Passenger Transport Executive. As part of this arrangement, 413 Midland Red buses were also transferred to the PTE with the majority eventually receiving the PTEs blue and cream livery. *Malcolm Keeley*

Harpers fleet also had six Daimler Fleetline double-deckers which passed to Midland Red. Four had Northern Counties bodies whilst two, including 2233 (TRE 948L), had ECW bodywork. Two very similar ECW bodied Fleetlines, ordered by Harpers, were delivered to Midland Red as fleet numbers 439/440. Designated D14, these were to be the last double-deckers received by Midland Red. *Malcolm Keeley*

Whereas the Leyland National became the standard bus for Midland Red, the Plaxton Supreme-bodied Leopard, from 1975 until almost the end, became the standard coach and dual-purpose vehicle with just a small batch of Willowbrook-bodied Leopards in 1980 interrupting the continuity of supply. No 733 (WOC 733T), a 1978 CDP20, is a typical example of the Leyland/Plaxton combination. In April 1982 it was photographed at work in Great Malvern.
*Malcolm Keeley*

Numerically the last new vehicles to enter service with Midland Red were 25 National 2 buses delivered in 1980. These were part of a larger order truncated because of the company's financial position and shrinking requirement for vehicles. Numerically the last was No 831 (EON 831V) seen parked at St Margaret Bus Station in June 1982.
*Trevor Follows*

The final enigma in the Midland Red story regarded vehicle No 832. The solitary Leyland Tiger with Plaxton 51-seat coachwork was designated C25, and was received by Midland Red before the September 1981 split. However, it did not enter service until afterwards and was allocated to the Midland Red (Express) fleet. It is still, therefore, very much open to debate as to which was the last Midland Red vehicle! No 832 was photographed leaving Digbeth in July 1982. *Trevor Follows*

# Midland Red Summary Fleet List

| Fleet No (s) | Reg No (s) | Chassis | Body | Seating capacity | Entered service |
|---|---|---|---|---|---|
| **(ex Birmingham Motor Express Co Ltd, Hagley Road route 1905)** | | | | | |
| | O 264-269 | Milnes-Daimler 16/20hp | Milnes Car Co | O18/18R | 1904 |
| | O 1270-1278 | Milnes-Daimler 24hp | Birch | O18/12R | 1904/5 |
| | O 1279 | Thornycroft 24hp | ? | O18/12R | 1905 |
| | O 1280 | Dourkopp 18/20hp | ? | O18/12R | 1905 |
| | O 1281-1282 | Wolseley 20hp (2 cyl) | ? | O18/18R | 1905 |
| **(ex City of Birmingham Tramways Co Ltd, Harborne route 1905)** | | | | | |
| | O 1301-1304 | Dourkopp | ? | O??/??R | 1905 |
| | O 1283-1291 | Brush 'B' | ? | O18/18R | 1906 |
| **(Vehicles purchased by Birmingham District Power & Traction Co Ltd for use by BMMO Co Ltd )** | | | | | |
| 0-12 | O 8200-8212 | Tilling-Stevens TTA1 | Brush | O18/16R | 1912 |
| **(Vehicles purchased by Birmingham District Power & Traction Co Ltd for use by BMMO Co Ltd )** | | | | | |
| 13-36 | O 9913-9936 | Tilling-Stevens TTA2 | Brush | O18/16R | 1913 |
| 37-42 | O 9937-9942 | Tilling-Stevens TTA2 | Birch | B27R | 1913 |
| 43-48 | OA 343-348 | Tilling-Stevens TTA2 | Hora | B27F | 1913 |
| 49 | OA 2549 | Tilling-Stevens TTA2 | Brush (?) | O18/16R (?) | 1913 |
| 50-79 | OA 4550-4579 | Tilling-Stevens TS3 | Tilling | B29F | 1914 |
| 80-99 | OA 7080-7099 | Tilling-Stevens TS3 | Tilling/Brush | B29R | 1915 |
| 100-101 | OA 7100-7101 | Tilling-Stevens TTA2 | ? | O18/16R (?) | 1915 |
| 102 | OA 7102 | Tilling-Stevens TTA2 | Birch | B29R | 1915 |
| 103 | OA 7103 | Tilling-Stevens TS3 | Brush | B29F | 1916 |
| 104-121 | OB 1104-1121 | Tilling-Stevens TS3 | Brush | B29F | 1916 |
| **(ex North Warwickshire Motor Omnibus & Transport Co 1918)** | | | | | |
| ? | AC 26 | Tilling-Stevens TS3 | ? | d/d | 1914 |
| ? | AC 31 | Tilling-Stevens TTA2 | ? | d/d | 1914 |
| ? | AC 32 | Tilling-Stevens TS3 | ? | s/d | 1914 |
| ? | AC 33/43 | Tilling-Stevens TS3 | ? | d/d | 1914/16 |
| ? | E 1772 | Tilling-Stevens TTA2 | ? | ? | 1916 |
| ? | E 1843/4 | Tilling-Stevens TS3 | ? | ? | 1916 |
| **(ex Scottish Motor Traction Co Ltd 1918)** | | | | | |
| ? | S 4443 | Tilling-Stevens TS3 | Collett & McDonald | Ch32 | 1914 |
| ? | S 4444/5 | Tilling-Stevens TS3 | Scottish Motor Traction | Ch32 | 1914 |

| Fleet No (s) | Reg No (s) | Chassis | Body | Seating capacity | Entered service |
|---|---|---|---|---|---|
| 122-130 | OE 1122-1130 | Tilling-Stevens TS3 | Brush | B29F | 1919 |
| 131 | OE 1131 | Tilling-Stevens TS3 | Collett & McDonald | Ch32 | 1919 |
| 132-147 | OE 1132-1147 | Tilling-Stevens TS3 | Brush | B29F | 1919 |
| 148-155 | OE 3148-3155 | Tilling-Stevens TS3 | Brush | B29F | 1919 |
| 156-197 | OE 6156-6197 | Tilling-Stevens TS3 | B.R.C.W./ Strachan & Brown | B29F | 1920 |
| 198-236 | OH 1198-1236 | Tilling-Stevens TS3 | B.R.C.W./ Strachan & Brown | B29F | 1920 |

In 1920, 39 Tilling-Stevens vehicles were purchased from the War Department. Some may have operated as 'lorry-buses', some received 'bus bodies almost immediately whilst others served as lorries, with van bodies, only. They were nearly all subjected to considerable body changes, particularly up to 1926, and this list illustrates the first passenger-carrying bodies fitted to these vehicles. They were all allocated new or vacant registration numbers and these were also subject to change. Again, only the first known registered numbers are shown here.

| Fleet No (s) | Reg No (s) | Chassis | Body | Seating capacity | Entered service |
|---|---|---|---|---|---|
| 301-305 (?) | OE 7301-7305 | Tilling-Stevens TS3 | Taylor; Kilner & Brookes; Motor Hiring; SMT; SMT | All Ch32 | 1920 |
| 311/2/4-6 (?) | OE 7311/2/4-6 | Tilling-Stevens TS3 | Birch B27R; Tilling B29F; Hora B27F; Hora B27F; Tilling | B29F | 1920 |
| ? | O 9932 | Tilling-Stevens TS3 | Tilt Van | - | 1920 |
| ? | O 9934 | Tilling-Stevens TS3 | Tilling | B29F | 1920 |
| ? | OA 7102 | Tilling-Stevens TS3 | Brush | B29F | 1920 |
| ? | O 9933 | Tilling-Stevens TS3 | T.P.E. Van | - | 1920 |

Note - One further chassis was sold and delivered direct to Stevens; three further chassis were sold and delivered direct to Potteries (as EH 1861/8, 2786). O 9932 was ex Stevens; O 9934, OA 7102, O 9933 were ex Potteries as chassis only.

| Fleet No (s) | Reg No (s) | Chassis | Body | Seating capacity | Entered service |
|---|---|---|---|---|---|
| ? | OE 7307/11 AC 31, O 9941, OE 7313 | Tilling-Stevens TS3 | B.R.C.W. | B29F | 1920 |
| ? | OA 345/6/8 | Tilling-Stevens TS3 | Carlyle | KO22/29F | 1920 |
| ? | AC 26 | Tilling-Stevens TS3 | Tilt Van | - | 1920 |
| ? | OE 1142/3 | Tilling-Stevens TS3 | B.R.C.W; Strachan & Brown | B29F | 1920 |
| ? | OE 3148-50 | Tilling-Stevens TS3 | Tilling; Brush; Tilling | B29F | 1920 |
| 306 (?) | OE 7306 | Tilling-Stevens TS3 | B.R.C.W. | B29F | 1920 |

Note - There were six further vehicles, viz: Chassis 941/9, immediately sold to Potteries, as EH 1869/70. Chassis 496 and 948 - dismantled for spares by BMMO in June 1920. Two further chassis for which there is no record of registration numbers during 1920. However, by 1921 they were:

| Fleet No (s) | Reg No (s) | Chassis | Body | Seating capacity | Entered service |
|---|---|---|---|---|---|
| ? | OE 3151/5 | Tilling-Stevens TS3 | B.R.C.W. | B29F | 1920 |
| 306-307 | OE 7306-7307 | Ford T | Carlyle | Ch11 | 1921 |
| 237-241 | OK 1237-1241 | Tilling-Stevens FS | Carlyle | KO22/29F | 1922 |
| 308-310 | OK 1308-1310 | Tilling-Stevens TS3 | Startin | Ch32 | 1922 |
| 311 | OE 7311 | Tilling-Stevens TS3 | Startin | Ch32 | 1922 |
| 312-313 | OE 7312-7313 | Tilling-Stevens TS3 | B.R.C.W. | B29F | 1922 |

| Fleet No (s) | Reg No (s) | Chassis | Body | Seating capacity | Entered service |
|---|---|---|---|---|---|
| 318-323 | HA 2318-2323 | Garford 20hp | Davidson | Ch18 | 1922 |
| 324/7-9 | HA 2324/7-9 | Garford 20hp | Carlyle | B20F | 1922 |
| 325-326 | HA 2325-2326 | Garford 20hp | Carlyle | B15F | 1922 |
| - | HA 2330 | Garford 20hp | No body fitted | - | 1922 |
| 331 | HA 2331 | Garford 20hp | Carlyle | B24F | 1922 |
| 332 | HA 2332 | Tilling-Stevens TS4B | Strachan & Brown | B29F | 1922 |
| ? | O 9930 | Tilling-Stevens TS3 | T.P.E. Van | - | 1922 |
| ? | OA 7101 | Tilling-Stevens TS3 | Tilt Van | - | 1922 |
| 242-256 | HA 2242-2256 | Tilling-Stevens FS | Carlyle | KO22/29F | 1923 |
| ? | O 9935 | Tilling-Stevens TS3 | T.P.E. Van | - | 1923 |
| 330 | HA 2330 | SOS S | Brush | B32F | 1923 |
| ? | EH 2019 (?) | Tilling-Stevens TS3 | T.P.E. Van | - | 1923 |
| 333 | HA 2333 | SOS S | Brush | B32F | 1923 |
| 334-347 | HA 2334-2347 | SOS S (Tilling) | Brush | B32F | 1923 |
| 348 | HA 2348 | SOS S | Davidson | Ch32 | 1923 |
| 349-353 | HA 2349-2353 | SOS S (Tilling) | Davidson | Ch32 | 1923 |
| 31(?) | O 9931 | Tilling-Stevens TS3 | Tilling | B29F | 1923 |
| ? | OA 4556-8/72 | Tilling-Stevens TS3 | Tilling | B29F | 1923 |
| 49(?) | OA 2549 | Tilling-Stevens TS3 | Brush | B29F | 1923 |
| 44(?) | OA 344 | Tilling-Stevens FS | Carlyle | KO22/29F | 1924 |
| 257-276 | HA 2257-2276 | Tilling-Stevens FS | Carlyle | KO22/29F | 1924 |
| 354-358 | HA 2354-2358 | SOS S (Tilling) | Davidson | Ch32 | 1924 |
| 359-392 | HA 2359-2392 | SOS S (Tilling) | Brush | B32F | 1924 |
| 393-434 | HA 2393-2434 | SOS S | Carlyle/Brush | B32F | 1925 |
| 435-440 | HA 2435-2440 | SOS S | Davidson | Ch32 | 1925 |
| 441-499 | HA 2441-2499 | SOS S | Carlyle/Brush/Ransomes | B32F | 1925 |
| 500 | HA 2500 | SOS FS | Carlyle | B34F | 1925 |
| 501-508 | HA 3501-3508 | SOS S | Ransomes/Carlyle/Brush | B32F | 1925 |
| 509-512 | HA 3509-3512 | SOS S | Carlyle/Ransomes/Brush | B32F | 1926 |
| 513-530 | HA 3513-3530 | SOS FS | Davidson | Ch34 | 1926 |
| 531 | HA 3531 | SOS FS | Carlyle | B34F | 1926 |
| 532 | HA 3532 | SOS Q | Carlyle | B37F | 1926 |
| 533-595 | HA 3533-3595 | SOS FS | Brush | B34F | 1926 |
| 596-665 | HA 3596-3665 | SOS Q | Carlyle/Brush | B37F | 1927 |
| 666-671 | HA 3666-3671 | SOS QC | Carlyle | Ch30 | 1927 |
| 680-693 | HA 3680-3693 | SOS Q | Brush | B37F | 1927 |
| 695-718 | HA 3695-3718 | SOS Q | Brush | B37F | 1927 |
| 672-679 | HA 3672-3679 | SOS QC | Carlyle | Ch30 | 1928 |
| 694 | HA 3694 | SOS Q | Carlyle | B37F | 1928 |
| 719-800 | HA 3719-3800 | SOS QL | Brush | B37F | 1928 |
| 801-820 | HA 4801-4820 | SOS QL | Brush | B37F | 1928 |
| 821-835 | HA 4821-4835 | SOS QLC | Short | Ch29 | 1928 |
| 836-906 | HA 4836-4906 | SOS QL | Brush/Ransomes | B37F | 1928 |

| Fleet No (s) | Reg No (s) | Chassis | Body | Seating capacity | Entered service |
|---|---|---|---|---|---|
| 879-881 | HA 4879-4881 | SOS QLC 6-cylinder | Short | Ch29 | 1929 |
| 907-955 | HA 4907-4955 | SOS M | Carlyle/Brush/ Ransomes | B34F | 1929 |
| 994-999 | HA 4994-4999 | SOS XL | Carlyle | C30F | 1929 |
| 1-6 | HA 5001-5006 | SOS XL | Carlyle/Brush | C30F | 1929 |
| 16-42 | HA 5016-5042 | SOS QLC 6-cylinder | Short | Ch29 | 1929 |
| 956-993 | HA 4956-4993 | SOS XL | Brush | C30F | 1929/30 |
| 8-15 | HA 5008-5015 | SOS MM 4-cylinder | Ransomes | B34F | 1929/30 |

Note - The 'XL' class was unsuccessful and in 1930 were converted to 'MM' 6-cylinder buses with new or nearly new Ransomes B34F bodies from, or intended for, 'MM' 4-cylinder type chassis. They all received revised registration numbers after conversion (q.v.). Nos 999, 1-4 did not enter service as 'XL' vehicles. The bodies from these 'XL' coaches were fitted to new 'RR' chassis which also received the original 'XL' registration numbers (q.v.).
The 'MM' 4-cylinder class were all converted to 'IM4' type in 1930 and received new

Short B34F bodies and revised registration numbers. Nos 48-54 did not enter service as 'MM' type vehicles, nor were all of them actually built as this type.
The solitary 'COD' 6-cylinder vehicle was redesignated 'MM' 6-cylinder later in 1930. The 'COD' 4-cylinder vehicles of 1930 were all transformed into 'IM4' type with new Short B34F bodies in 1931. The original registration numbers were, however, retained after conversion (q.v.).

| Fleet No (s) | Reg No (s) | Chassis | Body | Seating capacity | Entered service |
|---|---|---|---|---|---|
| 7 | HA 5007 | SOS COD 6-cylinder | Carlyle | B34F | 1930 |
| 43-54 | HA 5043-5054 | SOS MM 4-cylinder | Ransomes | B34F | 1930 |
| 956-988 | HA 4956-4988 | SOS RR | Brush | C30F | 1930 |
| 991-999 | HA 4991-4999 | SOS RR | Brush | C30F | 1930 |
| 1-6 | HA 5001-5006 | SOS RR | Carlyle/Brush | C30F | 1930 |
| 7-15 | HA 5007-5015 | SOS MM 6-cylinder | Carlyle/Ransomes | B34F | 1930 |
| 43-84 | HA 5043-5084 | SOS MM 6-cylinder | Ransomes | B34F | 1930 |
| 85-122 | HA 5085-5122 | SOS IM4 | Carlyle/Short | B34F | 1930 |
| 123 | HA 5123 | SOS BRR | Carlyle | DP34F | 1930 |
| 124 | HA 5124 | SOS COD 4-cylinder | Brush | B34F | 1930 |
| 125-134 | HA 5125-5134 | SOS MM 6-cylinder | Ransomes | B34F | 1930 |
| 135-145 | HA 5135-5145 | SOS QLC 6-cylinder | Short | Ch29 | 1930 |
| 146-152 | HA 6146-6152 | SOS QLC 6-cylinder | Short | Ch29 | 1930 |
| 153-173 | HA 6153-6173 | SOS COD 4-cylinder | Brush | B34F | 1930 |
| 174-175 | HA 6174-6175 | SOS SRR | Short | C30F | 1930 |
| (ex Great Western Railway 1930) | | | | | |
| ? | UU 4814 | Maudslay ML3A | Vickers | B32F | 1929 |
| ? | YU 4106/7 | Maudslay ML3A | Buckingham; Vickers | B32F | 1927 |
| ? | RF 3348 | Maudslay ML3A | Buckingham | C32F | 1927 |
| ? | RF 2457/869 | Maudslay ML | Buckingham | B26F | 1926/7 |
| ? | RF 4964 | Leyland TS1 | Leyland | B30F | 1928 |
| ? | YE 7310 | Guy FBB | Buckingham | B32F | 1927 |
| 124 | HA 5124 | SOS IM4 | Short | B34F | 1931 |
| 153-173 | HA 6153-6173 | SOS IM4 | Short | B34F | 1931 |
| 176-226 | HA 6176-6226 | SOS IM4 | Short | B34F | 1931 |
| 227-245 | HA 6227-6245 | SOS IM6 | Brush | B34F | 1931 |
| 326-328 | HA 7326-7328 | SOS IM6 | Brush | B34F | 1931 |
| 329 | HA 7329 | SOS REDD | Short | H22/26R | 1931 |

| Fleet No (s) | Reg No (s) | Chassis | Body | Seating capacity | Entered service |
|---|---|---|---|---|---|
| 246-295 | HA 8246-8295 | SOS IM4 | Brush/Metro-Cammell | B34F | 1932 |
| 1001-1025 | HA 8001-8025 | SOS REDD | Short/Eastern Counties | H26/26R | 1932 |
| 1026-1050 | HA 8026-8050 | SOS REDD | Brush/Metro-Cammell | H26/26R | 1932/3 |
| 296-323 | HA 8296-8323 | SOS IM6 | Short | B34F | 1933 |
| 324-325 | HA 8324-8325 | SOS IM4 | Short | B34F | 1933 |
| 1000 | HA 9000 | SOS FEDD | Carlyle | H26/26F | 1933 |
| 51(?) | HA 9051 | SOS LRR | Short | C30F | 1933 |
| 348-357 | HA 8348-8357 | SOS IM4 | Short | B34F | 1933/4 |
| 358-375 | HA 9358-9375 | SOS IM4 | Short | B34F | 1933/4 |
| 376-395 | HA 9376-9395 | SOS BRR | Short | B34F | 1934 |
| 396-400 | HA 9396-9400 | SOS LRR | Short | C30F | 1934 |
| 401-450 | HA 9401-9450 | SOS FEDD | Short | H30/26F | 1934 |
| 451-480 | HA 9451-9480 | SOS ON | Short | B38F | 1934 |
| 481 | HA 9481 | SOS DON | Short | B36F | 1934 |
| 482-483 | HA 9482-9483 | SOS ON | Short | B38F | 1934 |
| 484-485 | HA 9484-9485 | SOS DON | Short | B36F | 1934 |
| 486 | HA 9486 | SOS ON | Short | B38F | 1934 |

Note - The 'DON' type was an 'ON' type chassis fitted with an AEC 7.7 litre oil engine in place of the SOS 6-cylinder petrol unit which, because of the extra length of the diesel unit, required a longer bonnet and cab with the resultant loss of two passenger seats.

The 'CON' type (q.v.) were vehicles converted to use the BMMO 'K' type oil engine in place of the original petrol unit.

| Fleet No (s) | Reg No (s) | Chassis | Body | Seating capacity | Entered service |
|---|---|---|---|---|---|
| 487-536 | AHA 487-536 | SOS DON | Short | B38F | 1934/5 |
| 537-575 | AHA 537-575 | SOS DON | Short | B36F | 1935 |
| 576 | AHA 576 | SOS SON (Petrol) | Short | B38F | 1935 |
| 577-586 | AHA 577-586 | SOS DON | Brush | B36F | 1935 |
| 587-611 | AHA 587-611 | SOS LRR | Short | C30F | 1935 |
| 612-636 | AHA 612-636 | SOS OLR | Short | C29F | 1935 |

Note - BHA 1 was an experimental rear-engined bus converted to side-underfloor engine, as S1 type, in 1941. CHA 1 was a rear-engined coach converted to side-underfloor engine, as S2 type, in 1942 with body from CHA 2. CHA 2 was a rear-engined bus converted to side-underfloor engine, as S3 type, in 1943 with body from CHA 3. Also fitted with a Wilson preselector gearbox. CHA 3 was a rear-engined bus converted to side-underfloor engine, as S4 type, in 1944 with a new Carlyle B40F body.

| Fleet No (s) | Reg No (s) | Chassis | Body | Seating capacity | Entered service |
|---|---|---|---|---|---|
| 1 | BHA 1 | SOS REC | Carlyle | B40F | 1936 |
| 301-400 | BHA 301-400 | SOS FEDD | Metro-Cammell | H30/26F | 1936 |
| 801-835 | BHA 801-835 | SOS FEDD | Metro-Cammell | H30/26F | 1936 |
| 1 | CHA 1 | SOS REC | Carlyle | C32C | 1936 |
| 2 | CHA 2 | SOS REC | Carlyle | B40F | 1936 |
| 501-565 | CHA 501-565 | SOS SON | English Electric | B39F | 1936 |

(ex Leicester and District Bus Co Ltd 1936)

| | | | | | |
|---|---|---|---|---|---|
| ? | RY 8687 | Albion PR28 | London Lorries | C32R | 1936 |
| ? | JF 187/8/335 | Albion PMB28 | London Lorries | C32R | 1936 |
| ? | JF 4873/4 | Albion PV70 | Duple | C35F | 1936 |

| Fleet No (s) | Reg No (s) | Chassis | Body | Seating capacity | Entered service |
|---|---|---|---|---|---|
| 3 | CHA 3 | SOS REC | Carlyle | B40F | 1937 |
| 950-999 | CHA 950-999 | SOS SLR | English Electric | C30F | 1937 |
| 200 | DHA 200 | Dennis Lancet II | Short | B38F | 1937 |
| 637-736 | DHA 637-736 | SOS SON | English Electric | B38F | 1937/8 |
| 251-300 | EHA 251-300 | SOS FEDD | Brush | H30/26F | 1938 |
| 737-786 | EHA 737-786 | SOS SON | English Electric | B38F | 1938 |
| 201-221 | FHA 201-221 | SOS FEDD | Brush | H30/26F | 1938/9 |
| 200(?) | FHA 200 | SOS FEDD | Brush | H30/26F | 1939 |
| 223-250 | FHA 223-250 | SOS FEDD | Brush | H30/26F | 1939 |
| 401-425 | FHA 401-425 | SOS ONC | Duple | C30C | 1939 |
| 449-486 | FHA 449-486 | SOS SON | Brush | B38F | 1939 |
| 836-885 | FHA 836-885 | SOS FEDD | Brush | H30/26F | 1939 |
| 301-350 | GHA 301-350 | SOS SON | Brush | B38F | 1940 |
| | GHA 786-794 | Leyland Titan TD7 | Duple/N.C.M.E. | UH30/26R | 1942 |
| | GHA 795-800 | AEC Regent II | Brush | UH31/28R | 1942 |
| | GHA 886-891 | Guy Arab I | Weymann | UH30/26R | 1942 |

Note - In 1941/2, 44 SOS vehicles were received from the War Department at Slough or Ashchurch. All were formerly part of the Trent fleet and some were refurbished by Midland 'Red', entering service in 1942 or 1943.

| | | | | | |
|---|---|---|---|---|---|
| | CH 8904/5/10 | | | | |
| | CH 8911/6 | SOS COD 4-cylinder | Brush | B34F | |
| | CH 9900/1/5 | | | | |
| | CH 9907-11 | | | | |
| | CH 9913/4 | SOS IM6 | Short | B34F | |
| | CH 9917/9/21 | | | | |
| | CH 9925 | SOS IM4 | Short | B34F | |
| | RC 416/23 | SOS IM4 | Brush | B34F | |
| | RC 1281/2 | | | | |
| | RC 1291/5 | SOS IM4 | Short | B34F | |

CH 8904/5/10/1/6 were new in 1930 and formerly Trent Nos 204/5/10/1/6
CH 9900/1/5/7-11/3/4/7/9/21/5 were new in 1931 and formerly Trent Nos 120/1/5/7-31/3/4, 221/3/5/9
RC 416/23 were new in 1932 and formerly Trent Nos 241/8
RC 1281/2/91/5 were new in 1933 and formerly Trent Nos 262/3/72/6

The remaining 19 vehicles did not enter service with Midland Red, being broken up during 1942-44. For the sake of completeness these were: CH 8901/2/6/12/3 - COD 4-cylinder; CH 9902/6/12/5 - IM6; CH 9920/3/6/7, RC 411/7, 1285/96-8 - IM4

| | | | | | |
|---|---|---|---|---|---|
| | GHA 921-932 | Guy Arab II | Weymann/Metro-Cammell | UH30/26R | 1942 |
| | GHA 933-946 | Daimler CWA6 | Weymann/Duple | UH30/26R | 1943 |

In 1943 a further series of SOS vehicles was received from the War Department; this time from Sheffield. All originated in the Northern or Tynemouth fleets but none was placed in service by Midland 'Red', being returned to Northern General the same year. They were: CN 2878, SOS Q, formerly Northern 329, chassis No 453; UP 568 and FT 1884, SOS QL, formerly Northern 355 and Tynemouth 34, chassis Nos 665 and 777; BR 7021 and CU 2423, SOS M, formerly Northern 432/58, chassis Nos 979 and 1084; CN 4248, SOS SRR, formerly Northern 481, chassis No 1400; CN 5478, SOS IM6, formerly Northern 583, chassis No 1717.

*The following vehicles, delivered before March 1944 and still in stock, received at this time the 'A' or Private Identification Number as a Fleet Number.*

| Reg No (s) | New Fleet No (s) |
|---|---|
| HA 3779/81 | 857/62 |
| HA 4080/9/41/8 | 885/6, 902/23 |
| HA 4852/7/9/74/5 | 936/49/8/64/5 |
| HA 4892/3/7, 903 | 927/18/33/9 |
| HA 4909-13/5-29 | 972/56/70/1/3/5-81/8/2-7/9 |
| HA 4931-55 | 1022/3/5-8/4/01/29-44, 952 |
| HA 5007-15 | 1088/5/75/81/3, 1136, 1084/54/65 |
| HA 5043-101/3/4 | 1067/58/60/1/3/90/1/2/5/87/64/9/49/51/78/48/56/72/62/77 |
|  | 1076/0/80/66/79/86/73/52/68/47,1139-41, 1045, 1142-4 |
|  | 1046/50, 1145, 1071/93, 1116/09/11/0/01/12-5/7/23/4/18/21 |
|  | 1119/20/2/31/2 |
| HA 5106/8-34 | 1125/9/30/27/34, 1099, 1104/6, 1097, 1102/8/3/7, 1098, 1100 |
|  | 1096, 1246, 1147/38, 1094, 1137, 1055/3/7/9/74/89/2 |
| HA 6153-5/7/8 | 1148-50/2/3 |
| HA 6162-4/6-72 | 1157-9/62/3/1/6/5/7/8 |
| HA 6176-80/6-8 | 1247-51/7-9 |
| HA 6191/3/4/6/9 | 1262/4/5/8/74 |
| HA 6201/2/5-11 | 1279/67/76/0/7/8/80-2 |
| HA 6213-25 | 1284/8/5-7/9-96 |
| HA 6227-45 | 1297-9, 1301/2/3/0/4-15 |
| HA 7326-8 | 1316-8 |
| HA 7329 | 1319 |
| HA 8001/3-50 | 1370/5/7/80/2/4/7/6/9/92/3, 1403/7/5, 1371/6/8/9/83/5 |
|  | 1390/6/9, 1406, 1372/81/8/95/7/8, 1400/1/4/8/10/1/4/5/7 |
|  | 1373, 1402/9/12/3/6/8/, 1391/4, 1419 |
| HA 8246-52/4/5 | 1332/20-5/7/8 |
| HA 8257-60/2-7 | 1330/1/3/4/6-41 |
| HA 8269-95 | 1343/6/5/7-50/4/1-3/5/6/8/9/7/60-9/44 |
| HA 8296-306/8-23 | 1420-4/6/5/7/30/1/28/32-4/6/5/7-41/3/2/4-7 |
| HA 8324/5 | 1449/50 |
| HA 8349-51/3-7 | 1452-4/6/7/9/61/58 |
| HA 9000 | 1448 |
| HA 9051 | 1499 |
| HA 9358/61-4/6-75 | 1462/0/5-7/9-78 |
| HA 9376-95 | 1479-98 |
| HA 9396-400 | 1586-90 |
| HA 9401-50 | 1536-47/51/2/49/50/3-7/48/58-69/71/0/2-85 |
| HA 9451-86 | 1500-6/8/9/7/10-35 |
| AHA 487-586 | 1592-621/3/4/2/5-41/96, 1702/4-41, 1692-5/7, 1703, 1698/9 |
|  | 1700/1 |
| AHA 587-611 | 1642-66 |
| AHA 612-36 | 1668-76/67/77-91 |
| BHA 1 | 1591 |
| BHA 301-400 | 1744/3/2/5-8/50-8/60-8/71-5/80/8/9-826/749/59/69/70/6-9 |
|  | 1781-7/827-41 |
| BHA 801-835 | 1842-76 |
| CHA 1-3 | 1942-4 |
| CHA 501-65 | 1877-1941 |
| CHA 950-999 | 1968-2017 |
| DHA 637-736 | 2019-2118 |

An impressive array of Midland Red coaches in the late 1920s. *BaMMOT collection*

A mix of late prewar and early postwar types. *BaMMOT collection*

| Reg No (s) | FleetNo (s) |
|---|---|
| EHA 251-300 | 2119-2168 |
| EHA 737-786 | 2169-207/18/09-17/08 |
| FHA 201-21/00/3-50 | 2219-2268 |
| FHA 401-425 | 2269-2293 |
| FHA 449-486 | 2294-2331 |
| FHA 836-885 | 2332-2381 |
| GHA 301-350 | 2382-2431 |
| GHA 786-800 | 2432-2446 |
| GHA 886-891 | 2452-2457 |
| CH8904/5/10/1/6 | 2464/58/62/49/60 |
| CH 9900/1/5/7-11 | 2473/4/8/6/7/80-2 |
| CH 9913/4 | 2484/5 |
| CH 9917/9/21/5 | 2465/6/8/70 |
| RC 416/23 | 2488/9 |
| RC 1281/2/91/5 | 2490/1/3/4 |
| GHA 921-932 | 2497-2508 |
| GHA 933-946 | 2509-2522 |

*This is thought to be a complete list of all Midland Red buses numbered in March 1944. However, it is possible that there were others - at least HA 4816/37/8/63/76/83/4 existed, as ambulances, at the time although none was reinstated as a bus. HA 4809, shown above as No 886, was an ambulance until 1945 and withdrawn the same year. It may, therefore, not have been reinstated as a bus before withdrawal, nor received its new number. Finally, the first few of the HHA series of Guy Arabs were delivered around this time and it is possible, although unlikely, that they ran with 'bonnet numbers' for a very short time.*

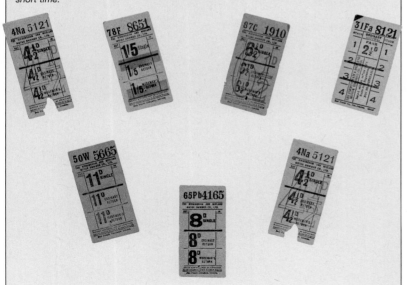

▲

A line-up of 16 C3 and C4 class coaches at Pensnett, a winter storage facility. *BaMMOT collection*

A mixture of D9s, DD12s and DD13s at Southgate Street Bus Garage, Leicester, in December 1979. *Mike Greenwood*

▼

| Fleet No (s) | Reg No (s) | Chassis | Body | Seating capacity | Entered service |
|---|---|---|---|---|---|
| 2530-2540 | GHA 965-975 | Daimler CWA6 | Duple | UH30/26R | 1944 |
| 2550-2578 | HHA 2-30 | Guy Arab II | Weymann/Park Royal | UH30/26R | 1944 |
| 2541 | HHA 1 | BMMO D1 | Weymann | H30/26R | 1945 |
| 2542-2549 | GHA 992-999 | Daimler CWA6 | Brush | UH30/26R | 1945 |
| 2580-2585 | HHA 57-62 | Guy Arab II | Park Royal | UH30/26R | 1945 |
| 2586-2590 | HHA 81-85 | Guy Arab II | N.C.M.E. | UH30/26R | 1945 |
| 2579 | HHA 222 | BMMO S5 | Metro-Cammell | B40F | 1946 |
| 3000-3099 | HHA 601-700 | BMMO S6 | Brush/Metro-Cammell | B40F | 1946/7 |
| 3100-3199 | JHA 1-100 | AEC Regent II (AD2) | Brush/Metro-Cammell | H30/26RD | 1948/50 |
| 3200-3299 | JHA 800-899 | BMMO S8 | Metro-Cammell | B40F | 1948/9 |
| 3300-3344 | KHA 300-344 | BMMO C1 | Duple | C30C | 1948/9 |
| 3345-3356 | KHA 345-356 | BMMO C2 | Duple | C26C | 1950 |
| 3357-3440 | LHA 357-440 | BMMO S9 | Brush | B40F | 1949 |
| 3441 | LHA 441 | BMMO S9 Mk I | Brush | B40F | 1950 |
| 3442-3456 | LHA 442-456 | BMMO S9 | Brush | B40F | 1949/50 |
| 3457-3556 | MHA 457-556 | BMMO D5 | Brush | H30/26R | 1949/50 |
| 3557-3576 | MHA 57-76 | Guy Arab III (GD6) | Guy/Park Royal | H30/26R | 1949 |
| 3577-3693 | NHA 577-693 | BMMO S10 | Brush/Metro-Cammell | B40F | 1949/50 |
| 3694 | NHA 694 | BMMO S13 Mk I | Brush | B44F | 1950 |
| 3695-3702 | NHA 695-702 | BMMO S10 | Brush/Metro-Cammell | B40F | 1950 |
| 3703 | NHA 703 | BMMO S11 | Metro-Cammell | B40F | 1950 |
| 3704-3732 | NHA 704-732 | BMMO S10 | Brush/Metro-Cammell | B40F | 1950 |
| 3733-3776 | NHA 733-776 | BMMO S12 | Brush/Metro-Cammell | B44F | 1950/1 |
| 3777-3876 | NHA 777-876 | BMMO D5B | Brush | H30/26RD | 1950-52 |
| 3877-3878 | OHA 877-878 | BMMO S13 | Carlyle/Willowbrook | B44F | 1951 |
| 3879-3975 | OHA 879-975 | BMMO S13 | Carlyle/Brush/Nudd | DP40F | 1951-53 |
| 3976 | OHA 976 | Not built | | | |
| 3977 | OHA 977 | BMMO LA | Carlyle | B44F | 1951 |
| 3978-4077 | SHA 378-477 | Leyland PD2 (LD8) | Leyland | H30/26RD | 1952/3 |
| 4078-4177 | THA 78-177 | BMMO D7 | Metro-Cammell | H32/26RD | 1953/4 |
| 4178 | THA 778 | BMMO S14 | Carlyle | B44F | 1954 |
| 4179-4241 | UHA 179-241 | BMMO C3 | Willowbrook | C37C | 1954 |
| 4242-4253 | UHA 242-253 | BMMO C4 | Carlyle/Alexander | C32C | 1954 |
| 4254-4352 | UHA 254-352 | BMMO S14 | Carlyle | B44F | 1955/6 |
| 4353-4452 | VHA 353-452 | BMMO D7 | Metro-Cammell | H32/26RD | 1954/5 |
| 4453-4552 | XHA 453-552 | BMMO D7 | Metro-Cammell | H37/26RD | 1955-7 |
| 4553-4600 | 553-600 AHA | BMMO S14 | Carlyle | B44F | 1956/7 |
| 4601-4650 | 601-650 AHA | BMMO S15 | Carlyle | DP40F | 1957 |
| 4651-4652 | 651-652 AHA | BMMO S14 | Carlyle | B44F | 1957 |
| 4653-4721 | 653-721 BHA | BMMO S14 | Carlyle | B44F | 1957-9 |
| 4722 | 722 BHA | BMMO C5 | Carlyle | C37F | 1958 |
| 4723-4772 | 723-772 BHA | BMMO D7 | Metro-Cammell | H37/26RD | 1957 |
| 4773 | 773 FHA | BMMO D9 | Carlyle | H40/32RD | 1958 |
| 4774-4776 | 774-776 GHA | BMMO C5 | Carlyle | C37F | 1958 |
| 4777 | 799 GHA | BMMO C5 | Carlyle | C37F | 1958 |
| 4778-4798 | 778-798 GHA | BMMO C5 | Carlyle | C37F | 1958-60 |
| 4799 | 799 HHA | BMMO C5 | Carlyle | C37F | 1960 |

| Fleet No (s) | Reg No (s) | Chassis | Body | Seating capacity | Entered service |
|---|---|---|---|---|---|
| 4800-4815,<br>4826/30 | 800-815,<br>826/30 HHA | BMMO CM5/CM5T | Carlyle | C34F/C37F | 1960/1 |
| 4816-4825,<br>4827-4829,<br>4831-4837 | 816-825,<br>827-829,<br>831-837 HHA | BMMO C5 | Carlyle | C37F | 1961 |
| (ex Kemp & Shaw Ltd) | | | | | |
| 4838 | DJF 392 | Guy Arab II | N.C.M.E. | H30/26R | 1946 |
| 4839 | EBC 882 | Guy Arab III | N.C.M.E. | H30/26R | 1947 |
| 4840-4841 | EJF 668-669 | Guy Arab III | N.C.M.E. | H30/26R | 1948 |
| 4842-4843 | FJF 89-90 | Guy Arab III | Barnard | B35F | 1949 |
| 4844 | GRY 763 | Leyland PD2 | Leyland | L27/26R | 1950 |
| 4845 | JBC 989 | Leyland PD2 | Leyland | H30/26R | 1952 |
| (ex H. Boyer & Son, Rothley) | | | | | |
| 4846 | HAW 578 | Sentinel STC4 | Sentinel | B44F | 1951 |
| 4847 | GUT 543 | Sentinel STC6 | Sentinel | B44F | 1951 |
| 4848 | HJU 546 | Leyland PSU1 | Leyland | B44F | 1952 |
| 4849-4942 | 849-942 KHA | BMMO D9 | Carlyle | H40/32RD | 1960/1 |
| 4943 | 943 KHA | BMMO D10 Mk I | Carlyle | H43/35F | 1961 |
| 4944 | 1944 HA | BMMO D10 Mk II | Carlyle | H37/28D | 1961 |
| 4945-5044 | 2945-3044 HA | BMMO D9 | Carlyle | H40/32RD | 1961-3 |
| 5045-5092 | 5045-5092 HA | BMMO S15 | Carlyle | DP40F | 1962 |
| 5093 | 5093 HA | BMMO S19 | Carlyle | B52F | 1963 |
| 5094-5144 | 5094-5144 HA | BMMO S16 | Carlyle | B52F | 1962/3 |
| 5145-5174 | 5145-5174 HA | Leyland PSU3 (LS18) | Weymann/<br>Willowbrook | B53F | 1962/3 |
| 5175-5194 | 5175-5194 HA | Leyland PSU3 (LS18A) | Willowbrook | DP48F | 1963 |
| 5195-5244 | 5195-5244 HA | Leyland PSU3 (LS18) | Willowbrook | B53F | 1962/3 |
| 5245-5294 | 5245-5294 HA | Daimler CRG6 (DD11) | Alexander | H44/33F | 1963 |
| 5295 | 5495 HA | BMMO CM6T | Carlyle | C46F | 1963 |
| 5296-5378 | 6296-6378 HA | BMMO D9 | Carlyle | H40/32RD | 1963/4 |
| 5379-5394 | AHA 379-394B | BMMO D9 | Carlyle | H40/32RD | 1964 |
| 5395-5404 | BHA 395-404C | BMMO D9 | Carlyle | H40/32RD | 1965 |
| 5405-5445 | EHA 405-445D | BMMO D9 | Carlyle | H40/32RD | 1966 |
| 5446-5511 | 6446-6511 HA | BMMO S17 | Carlyle | B52F | 1963/4 |
| 5512-5545 | 6512-6545 HA | BMMO S16 | Carlyle | B52F | 1964 |
| 5546-5595 | AHA 146-195B | BMMO S17 | Carlyle | B52F | 1964 |
| 5596-5645 | BHA 596-645C | BMMO S17 | Carlyle | B52F | 1965 |
| 5646-5659 | BHA 646-659C | BMMO CM6T | Carlyle | C44F | 1965 |
| 5660-5665 | DHA 960-965C | BMMO CM6T | Carlyle | C44F | 1965 |
| 5667-5671 | EHA 667-671D | BMMO CM6 | Carlyle | C46F | 1966 |
| 5666/72-4 | EHA 666/72-4D | BMMO CM6T | Carlyle | C44F | 1966 |
| 5675-5700 | CHA 675-700C | BMMO S17 | Carlyle | B52F | 1965 |
| 5701-5721 | DHA 701-721C | BMMO S17 | Carlyle | B52F | 1965/6 |
| 5722-5724 | DHA 722-724C | BMMO S21A | Carlyle | DP48F | 1966 |
| 5725-5773 | EHA 725-773D | BMMO S17 | Carlyle | B52F | 1966 |
| 5774-5822 | CHA 74-122C | Leyland PSU3 (LC7) | Duple | C49F | 1965 |
| 5823 | CHA 123C | Leyland L2T (LC8) | Plaxton | C36F | 1965 |
| 5824-5838 | GHA 324-338D | Leyland PSU4 (LC9) | Plaxton | C36F | 1966 |
| 5839-5848 | JHA 839-848E | Leyland PSU3 (LS20) | Willowbrook | DP49F | 1966 |
| 5849-5868 | JHA 849-868E | BMMO S21 | Carlyle | DP49F | 1967 |

| Fleet No (s) | Reg No (s) | Chassis | Body | Seating capacity | Entered service |
|---|---|---|---|---|---|
| 5869-5878 | LHA 869-878F | BMMO S21 | Carlyle | DP49F | 1967 |
| 5879-5903 | MHA 879-903F | BMMO S22 | Carlyle | DP45F | 1968 |
| 5904-5915 | PHA 504-515G | BMMO S22 | Carlyle | DP45F | 1968 |
| 5916-5939 | RHA 916-939G | BMMO S23 | Carlyle | B51F | 1968/9 |
| 5940-5991 | UHA 940-991H | BMMO S23 | Carlyle | B51F | 1969/70 |
| 5992-6041 | GHA 392-441D | Daimler CRG6 (DD12) | Alexander | H44/33F | 1966/7 |
| 6042-6091 | JHA 42-91E | Daimler CRG6 (DD12) | Alexander | H44/33F | 1967 |
| 6092-6140 | LHA 592-640F | Daimler CRG6 (DD12) | Alexander | H44/33F | 1968 |
| 6141-6155 | SHA 641-655G | Leyland PSU4A (LC10) | Plaxton | C36F | 1969 |
| 6156-6190 | SHA 856-890G | Daimler CRG6 (DD13) | Alexander | H45/30D | 1969 |
| 6191-6225 | UHA 191-225H | Daimler CRG6 (DD13) | Alexander | H45/30D | 1969 |
| 6226-6255 | WHA 226-255H | Leyland PSU3A (LC11) | Plaxton | C49F | 1970 |
| **(ex Sheffield Transport 1970)** | | | | | |
| 6256-6260 | 6170-6174 WJ | Leyland L1 | Weymann | C41F | 1960 |
| 6261-6293 | YHA 261-293J | Daimler CRG6 (DD13) | Alexander | H45/30D | 1970/1 |
| 6294-6393 | YHA 294-393J | Ford R192 (S25 later F1) | Plaxton | B45F | 1970/1 |

*(Some of these vehicles were rebuilt as midibuses)*

| Fleet No (s) | Reg No (s) | Chassis | Body | Seating capacity | Entered service |
|---|---|---|---|---|---|
| **(ex Stratford-upon-Avon Blue Motors Ltd 1971)** | | | | | |
| 2001-2006 | 668-673 HNX | Leyland PD3A | Willowbrook | H41/32F | 1963 |
| 2007/2008 | GUE 1/2D | Leyland PD3A | Willowbrook | H41/32F | 1966 |
| 2009-2011 | NAC 415-417F | Leyland PDR1 | Northern Counties | H44/31F | 1967 |
| 2020 | TNX 454 | Leyland PD2 | Willowbrook | H35/28RD | 1956 |
| 2024-2027 | 536-539 EUE | Leyland PD3 | Northern Counties | H41/32F | 1963 |
| 2028-2030 | 2767-2769 NX | Leyland PD3 | Willowbrook | H41/32F | 1960 |
| 2031-2035 | AUE 309-313J | Leyland PSUR1 | Marshall | B41D | 1970 |
| 2036 | XNX 136H | Leyland PSUR1 | Alexander | C49F | 1970 |
| 2040-2043 | 2741-2744 AC | Leyland PSU3A | Willowbrook | DP41F | 1959 |
| 2044 | 2745 AC | Leyland PSUC1 | Willowbrook | B45F | 1959 |
| 2045-2048 | 3945-3948 UE | Leyland PSUC1 | Park Royal | B45F | 1960 |
| 2049 | 5449 WD | Leyland PSUC1 | Marshall | B43F | 1962 |
| 2050-2052 | 5450-5452 WD | Leyland PSUC1 | Marshall | DP41F | 1962 |
| 2053 | 5455 WD | Leyland PSUC1 | Marshall | DP41F | 1962 |
| 2054 | CWD 33C | Leyland PSU3 | Weymann | B53F | 1965 |
| 2055 | 436 GAC | Leyland PSU3 | Duple | C49F | 1963 |
| 2056/2057 | AAC 21/22B | Leyland L2T | Marshall | DP41F | 1964 |
| 2058 | DAC 753C | Leyland PSU3 | Duple | C49F | 1965 |
| 2059 | HAC 628D | Leyland PSU4 | Marshall | DP41F | 1966 |
| 2132-2135 | JUE 348-351 | Leyland PD2 | Northern Counties | H35/28F | 1950 |

*(Nos 2031-2035, although repainted red, were not operated by Midland Red)*

| Fleet No (s) | Reg No (s) | Chassis | Body | Seating capacity | Entered service |
|---|---|---|---|---|---|
| 6394-6399 | YHA 394-399J | Leyland PSU3A (S24) | Willowbrook | DP49F | 1971 |
| 6400 | YHA 499J | Leyland PSU3A (S24) | Willowbrook | DP49F | 1971 |
| 6401-6416 | YHA 401-416J | Leyland PSU3A (S24) | Willowbrook | DP49F | 1971 |
| 6417-6445 | CHA 417-445K | Leyland PSU3A (S24) | Willowbrook | DP49F | 1971 |
| 6446-6453 | AHA 446-453J | Leyland PSU4B (C12) | Plaxton | C40F | 1971 |
| 6454-6460 | CHA 454-460K | Leyland PSU4B (C12) | Plaxton | C40F | 1971 |
| 6461-6473 | DHA 461-473K | Leyland PSU3A (S26) | Marshall | B53F | 1972 |
| 101-158 | HHA 101-158L | Leyland 1151 (N1) | Leyland | B51F | 1972/3 |
| 159-178 | HHA 159-178L | Ford R1014 (F2) | Plaxton | B45F | 1972 |
| 179-190 | HHA 179-190L | Leyland PSU4B (C12) | Plaxton | C40F | 1972/73 |
| 191-198 | HHA 191-198L | Leyland PSU3B (C13) | Plaxton | C44F/C48F | 1973 |
| 199-248 | JHA 199-248L | Leyland PSU3B (S27) | Marshall | DP49F | 1973 |
| 249-298 | NHA 249-298M | Leyland 1151 (N2) | Leyland | B49F/B51F | 1973/4 |

**(ex G. Cooper & Sons, Oakengates 1973)**

| Fleet No (s) | Reg No (s) | Chassis | Body | Seating capacity | Entered service |
|---|---|---|---|---|---|
| 2136 | WAW 502 | Bedford SB1 | Duple | C41F | 1961 |
| 2137/2138 | DAW 825/826C | Bedford VAL14 | Plaxton | C41F | 1965 |
| 2139 | DUJ 549C | Bedford SB5 | Plaxton | C41F | 1965 |
| 2140/2141 | FAW 156/157D | Bedford VAM5 | Willowbrook | B45F | 1966 |
| 2142/2143 | LAW 30/31F | Bedford VAM70 | Duple | C45F | 1968 |
| 2144 | UUJ 447J | Bedford YRQ | Willowbrook | B45F | 1971 |
| 2145 | VNT 848J | Bedford YRQ | Willowbrook | B45F | 1971 |
| 2146 | WUX 656K | Bedford YRQ | Duple | C45F | 1971 |
| 2147 | XUX 558K | Bedford YRQ | Duple | C45F | 1972 |
| 2148 | CAW 135L | Bedford YRT | Plaxton | C53F | 1973 |

*(Nos 2136-2139 not operated by Midland Red)*

**(ex Green Bus Co Ltd, Rugeley 1973)**

| Fleet No (s) | Reg No (s) | Chassis | Body | Seating capacity | Entered service |
|---|---|---|---|---|---|
| 2149 | WDG 379J | Seddon Pennine VI | Plaxton | C53F | 1971 |
| 2150 | HRE 683K | Seddon Pennine VI | Plaxton | C55F | 1972 |
| 2151 | TBU 598G | Seddon Pennine RU | Seddon | B43D | 1969 |
| 2152/2153 | YRF 136/137H | Seddon Pennine IV | Pennine | B42F | 1969 |
| 2154 | FRF 762K | Seddon Pennine IV | Seddon | B42F | 1972 |
| 2155 | MRF 393L | Seddon Pennine VI | Willowbrook | C47F | 1972 |
| 2156 | NRF 887L | Seddon Pennine VI | Willowbrook | C47F | 1972 |
| 2157/2158 | RRE 862/863L | Seddon Pennine VI | Willowbrook | C53F | 1973 |
| 2159 | XHW 419 | Bristol LS5G | ECW | B45F | 1957 |
| 2160 | YHY 79 | Bristol LS5G | ECW | B45F | 1957 |
| 2161 | MAX 107 | Bristol LS6G | ECW | B45F | 1954 |
| 2162 | YHY 81 | | ECW | B45F | 1958 |
| 2163/2164 | 330/331 RBF | | Duple | C41F | 1963 |
| 2165 | 4778 NE | | Duple | C41F | 1963 |
| 2166 | KRE 625B | Fo | Duple | C41F | 1964 |

| Fleet No (s) | Reg No (s) | Chassis | Body | Seating capacity | Entered service |
|---|---|---|---|---|---|
| 2167 | 1375 VC | Ford 570E | Duple | C41F | 1962 |
| 2168 | 1856 VC | Ford 570E | Duple | C41F | 1962 |
| 2169 | 88 EYY | AEC Reliance | Plaxton | C45F | 1963 |
| 2170 | 44 AUW | AEC Reliance | Willowbrook | C41F | 1961 |
| 2171 | VFM 596 | Bristol LD6B | ECW | H33/25RD | 1955 |
| 2172 | VFM 620 | Bristol LD6B | ECW | H33/27RD | 1955 |
| 2173 | VFM 624 | Bristol LD6B | ECW | H33/27RD | 1955 |
| 2174 | RFM 435 | Bristol LD6B | ECW | H33/25R | 1954 |
| 2175 | 504 BRM | Bristol FSF6B | ECW | H34/26F | 1960 |
| 2176 | 501 BRM | Bristol FSF6B | ECW | H34/26F | 1960 |
| 2177 | LJX 18 | AEC Regent V | Metro-Cammell | H40/32F | 1960 |

*(Nos 2159-2177 not operated by Midland Red)*

**(ex T. Hoggins & Sons, Wrockwardine Wood 1974)**

| Fleet No (s) | Reg No (s) | Chassis | Body | Seating capacity | Entered service |
|---|---|---|---|---|---|
| 2178 | PRA 249E | Bedford VAM14 | Duple | C45F | 1967 |
| 2179 | SAB 468F | Bedford VAM70 | Duple | C45F | 1968 |
| 2180 | RTJ 364G | Ford R192 | Plaxton | C45F | 1969 |
| 2181 | XUX 417K | Ford R192 | Plaxton | B47F | 1972 |
| 2182 | AAW 471K | Ford R1014 | Plaxton | C45F | 1972 |

*(Nos 2178-2180/2182 not operated by Midland Red)*

| Fleet No (s) | Reg No (s) | Chassis | Body | Seating capacity | Entered service |
|---|---|---|---|---|---|
| 299-318 | PHA 299-318M | Leyland PSU3B (C14) | Plaxton | C44FT | 1974 |
| 319-338 | PHA 319-338M | Leyland PSU3B (S28) | Marshall | DP49F | 1974 |
| 339 | SHA 639N | Leyland PSU3B (S28) | Marshall | DP49F | 1974 |
| 340-349 | GJW 40-49N | Leyland PSU3B (S28) | Marshall | DP49F | 1974 |
| 350-361 | GOH 350-361N | Leyland PSU3B (S28) | Marshall | DP49F | 1974 |
| 362-368 | GOL 362-368N | Leyland PSU3B (S28) | Marshall | DP49F | 1975 |
| 369-388 | PHA 369-388M | Ford R1014 (F3) | Plaxton | B45F | 1974 |

*(Some of these vehicles were rebuilt as midibuses)*

| Fleet No (s) | Reg No (s) | Chassis | Body | Seating capacity | Entered service |
|---|---|---|---|---|---|
| 389-391 | PHA 489-491M | Leyland 11351 (N3) | Leyland | B49F | 1974 |
| 392-438 | GOL 392-438N | Leyland 11351 (N3) | Leyland | B49F | 1974/5 |

**(ex Harper Brothers [Heath Hayes] Ltd 1974)**

| Fleet No (s) | Reg No (s) | Chassis | Body | Seating capacity | Entered service |
|---|---|---|---|---|---|
| 2201 | JXN 349 | Leyland 7RT | Park Royal | H30/26R | 1948 |
| 2203 | OLD 820 | Leyland 7RT | Park Royal | H30/26R | 1954 |
| 2204 | KXW 284 | Leyland 7RT | Weymann | H30/26R | 1950 |
| 2207 | KYY 770 | Leyland 7RT | Metro-Cammell | H30/26R | 1950 |
| 2208 | BDJ 802 | AEC Regent III | Park Royal | H30/26R | 1951 |
| 2209 | BDJ 807 | AEC Regent III | Park Royal | H30/26RD | 1951 |
| 2211 | 888 DUK | Guy Arab V | | H41/31F | 1963 |
| 2222 | 1031 E | Leyland PSU1 | | DP41F | 1953 |
| 2223 | NRF 349F | Leyland PD3A | | H40/32RD | 1968 |
| 2224 | LRF 992F | Leyland PD3A | | H40/32RD | 1968 |

| Fleet No (s) | Reg No (s) | Chassis | Body | Seating capacity | Entered service |
|---|---|---|---|---|---|
| 2225 | SBF 233 | Leyland PD2 | Northern Counties | H36/28RD | 1962 |
| 2226 | LRF 993F | Leyland PD3A | Northern Counties | H40/32RD | 1968 |
| 2227/2228 | HBF 679/680D | Leyland PD2A | Metro-Cammell | H36/28RD | 1966 |
| 2229/2230 | JBF 405/406H | Daimler CRG6LX | Northern Counties | H44/33F | 1970 |
| 2231/2232 | BRE 311/312J | Daimler CRG6LX | Northern Counties | H44/31F | 1971 |
| 2233/2234 | TRE 948/949L | Daimler CRL6 | ECW | H43/31F | 1973 |
| 2247 | NRF 420L | Bedford SB5 | Willowbrook | B40F | 1972 |
| 2248/2249 | VRF 629/630 | Leyland PSU1 | Harper | DP44F | 1951 |
| 2250 | XRE 725 | Leyland PSU1 | Burlingham | DP41F | 1952 |
| 2251 | LRF 220K | Leyland PSU4B | Duple | C45F | 1972 |
| 2252/2253 | MRF 417/418L | Leyland PSU3B | Duple | C51F | 1972 |
| 2257/2258 | ARE 710/711J | Bedford SB5 | Duple | C41F | 1971 |
| 2259/2260 | 1293/1294 RE | Guy Arab LUF | Burlingham | C41F | 1959 |
| 2261 | SBF 447J | Leyland PSU3 | Plaxton | C51F | 1970 |
| 2262 | FBF 794H | Bedford VAM70 | Duple | C45F | 1970 |
| 2263 | FBF 791H | Bedford VAM70 | Duple | C45F | 1970 |
| 2264 | SBF 218J | Leyland PSU3 | Plaxton | C51F | 1970 |
| 2265 | OBF 593J | Bedford VAM70 | Duple | C45F | 1970 |
| 2266 | LBF 663H | Bedford VAM70 | Duple | C45F | 1970 |
| 2267 | PBF 199M | Leyland PSU5 | Plaxton | C55F | 1973 |
| 2268/2269 | ORF 457/458F | Leyland PSU3 | Duple | C51F | 1968 |
| 2270 | VRE 698G | Bedford SB5 | Duple | C41F | 1969 |
| 2271/2272 | ARE 712/713J | Bedford SB5 | Duple | C41F | 1971 |
| 2273 | WRE 336G | Bedford SB5 | Duple | C41F | 1969 |
| 2274 | FBF 793H | Bedford VAM70 | Duple | C45F | 1970 |
| ?275/2276 | ORF 459/460F | Leyland PSU3 | Duple | C51F | 1968 |
| ? | FBF 792H | Bedford VAM70 | Duple | C45F | 1970 |
| ? | SBF 217J | Leyland PSU3 | Plaxton | C51F | 1970 |

(?204/2207/2208/2248/2250 not operated by Midland Red)

(... s/Tudor Rose Coaches Ltd, Sutton Coldfield 1974)

| Fleet No (s) | Reg No (s) | Chassis | Body | Seating capacity | Entered service |
|---|---|---|---|---|---|
| 22? | MRF 419L | Leyland PSU3B | Duple | C51F | 1972 |
| 2255/?? | MRF 420/421L | Leyland PSU4B | Duple | C45F | 1972 |
| 439/440 | JOX 439/440P | Daimler CRG6 (D14) | ECW | H43/31F | 1976 |
| 441-449 | JOX 441-449P | Leyland PSU3C (C15) | Plaxton | C47F | 1975/76 |

(Nos 441-443 not operated by Midland Red)

| Fleet No (s) | Reg No (s) | Chassis | Body | Seating capacity | Entered service |
|---|---|---|---|---|---|
| 450-470 | JOX 450-470P | Leyland PSU3C (CDP16) | Plaxton | C49F | 1976 |
| 471-501 | JOX 471-501P | Leyland 11351 (N4) | Leyland | B49F | 1975/76 |
| 502-535 | JOX 502-535P | Leyland 11351A (N5) | Leyland | B49F | 1976 |
| 536-610 | NOE 536-610R | Leyland 11351A (N6) | Leyland | B49F | 1976/7 |
| 611-616 | NOE 611-616R | Leyland PSU3D (C17) | Plaxton | C47F | 1976/7 |

| Fleet No (s) | Reg No (s) | Chassis | Body | Seating capacity | Entered service |
|---|---|---|---|---|---|
| 617-656 | PUK 617-656R | Leyland 11351A (N7) | Leyland | B49F | 1977/8 |
| 657-664 | SOA 657-664S | Leyland 11351A (N7) | Leyland | B49F | 1977 |

**(ex London Country Bus Services Ltd 1977)**

| | | | | | |
|---|---|---|---|---|---|
| 2121/2122 | VPF 121-122M | Ford Transit (M1) | Dormobile | B16F | 1974 |
| 2123-2125 | XPE 123-125N | Ford Transit (M1) | Dormobile | B16F | 1974 |

*(Nos 2121/2124/2123 were originally numbered 441-443)*

| | | | | | |
|---|---|---|---|---|---|
| 665-670 | RDA 665-670R | Leyland PSU3E (CDP18) | Plaxton | C49F | 1977 |
| 671-682 | SOA 671-682S | Leyland PSU3E (CDP18) | Plaxton | C49F | 1977/8 |
| 683-719 | TOF 683-719S | Leyland 11351A (N8) | Leyland | B49F | 1978 |
| 720-724 | WOC 720-724T | Leyland 11351A (N8) | Leyland | B49F | 1978 |
| 725-729 | WOC 725-729T | Leyland PSU3E (C19) | Plaxton | C46F | 1978 |
| 730-741 | WOC 730-741T | Leyland PSU3E (CDP20) | Plaxton | C49F | 1978/9 |

**(ex Potteries Motor Traction 1979)**

| | | | | | |
|---|---|---|---|---|---|
| 2790 | 790 EVT | Leyland PDR1 | Weymann | L39/34F | 1959 |
| 2825 | 825 KVT | Leyland PDR1 | Weymann | L39/34F | 1960 |
| 2905 | 905 UVT | Leyland PDR1 | Weymann | L39/33F | 1962 |
| 2907 | 907 UVT | Leyland PDR1 | Weymann | L39/33F | 1962 |
| 2910 | 910 UVT | Leyland PDR1 | Weymann | L39/33F | 1962 |
| 2972 | 972 XVT | Daimler CRG6LX | Northern Counties | H40/33F | 1963 |
| 2974 | 974 XVT | Daimler CRG6LX | Northern Counties | H40/33F | 1963 |

*(Nos 2790/2825/2905/2907/2972/2974 not operated by Midland Red)*

**(ex National Travel [West] 1979)**

| | | | | | |
|---|---|---|---|---|---|
| 2591 | CDH 145T | Bedford YMT | Plaxton | C53F | |
| 2592-2600 | YUE 592-600S | Bedford YMT | Plaxton | C53F | |
| 2601-2602 | VDH 243/244S | Leyland PSU3E/4 | Willowbrook | C28F | |

*(Nos 2592-2597/2601-2602 were only loaned to Midland Red)*

| | | | | | |
|---|---|---|---|---|---|
| 742-760 | XOV 742-760T | Leyland 11351A (N9) | Leyland | B49F | 1979 |
| 761-773 | BVP 761-773V | Leyland 11351A (N9) | Leyland | B49F | 1979/80 |
| 774-783 | BVP 774-783V | Leyland PSU3E (C21) | Plaxton | C53F | 1979/80 |
| 784-788 | BVP 784-788V | Leyland PSU3E (CDP23) | Plaxton | C53F | 1980 |
| 789-806 | BVP 789-806V | Leyland PSU3E (CDP22) | Willowbrook | C53F | 1980 |
| 807-822 | BVP 807-822V | Leyland NL116L11 (N10) | Leyland | B49F | 1980 |
| 823-831 | EON 823-831V | Leyland NL116L11 (N10) | Leyland | B49F | 1980 |
| 832 | LOA 832X | Leyland TRCTL11 (C25) | Plaxton | C51F | 1981 |